God Made Organics,
Not GMOs

...SOOO,
WTF IS
IN FOOD TODAY?

Karen vanPrice

ISBN - 978-0-692-46467-0

*This book is dedicated to my family and friends -
those who believe what I write and those who don't.
I have learned much from both sides and know
that the yin and yang of life requires me to appreciate
opposition for the lessons and fruit it bears.*

*"It is health that is real wealth and
not pieces of gold and silver."*
- Mahatma Gandhi

Foreword

The quality of our food is a topic that interests us all. Author Karen vanPrice has a mission to inform her readers that the food they eat may not be what it seems. More importantly she offers a down-to-earth, "I'm just one person trying to help another" enlightening guide to help you become an informed and educated food consumer.

If you've ever wondered why so many people suffer from food sensitivities and allergies, it's because our food supply has undergone a recent radical change. In the mid-1990's, new food proteins were engineered and introduced into our food supply, unannounced and untested on humans and animals.

These genetically modified organisms (GMOs) have had their genetic code (DNA) altered to give them characteristics they don't naturally have.

In an effort to increase production and profits for food manufacturers, scientists artificially insert bacteria, viruses and other genes into the DNA of soy, corn, canola, sugar beets, cottonseed and many other foods. A genetically engineered growth hormone, rBGH (recombinant bovine growth hormone) is used on dairy cows.

As crazy as it sounds, there have never been any human clinical trials on the effects of GMOs on our health, and not many long-term animal-feeding studies either, so we are largely in the dark about their effect on living creatures, including humans.

In 2009, the American Academy of Environmental Medicine (AAEM) stated, "Several animal studies indicate serious health risks associated with genetically modified (GM) food," including infertility, immune problems, accelerated aging, faulty insulin regulation, and changes in major organs and the gastrointestinal system. The AAEM has asked physicians to advise all patients to avoid GMO foods.

Has your doctor ever told you to avoid GMO foods?? Probably not. That's why God Made Organics, Not GMOs is such an important book.

Karen Price has written from her heart. She is a passionate and fearless woman. Her friendly and down-to-earth demeanor makes her relatable and approachable. Having had the pleasure and privilege to be interviewed by Karen on the topic of GMOs, I can attest that she is someone you want by your side. Not only does she write from a place of knowledge and experience, she personifies health and holds a deep enjoyment for helping others achieve their own health goals.

God Made Organics, Not GMOs is a clear and concise approach to help readers navigate the grocery store and learn to enjoy the benefits of eating healthy foods. She has left no stone unturned when it comes to the dangers of GMOs and the benefits of organic foods. Her book answers all of the questions you may have about how to get started on a non-GMO lifestyle, while also offering ideas for those who have already made the transition.

What I appreciate most about this book is the unwavering message that our bodies are not designed to eat food that has been altered by science. Whether you have food sensitivities or not, avoiding processed and GMO foods should be a priority. We can't wait for legislation. We must begin to act in our own self-interest.

If you want to truly take charge of your health and the health of your loved ones, *God Made Organics, Not GMOs* is the book for you. This outstanding, easy-to-follow guide will not only bring you closer to achieving your health goals, but the health of future generations.

It may sound exaggerated, but genetically modified foods are, from my perception, one of the most significant health threats of our time. Everything you can do to avoid GMOs is a step toward saving humankind. Karen vanPrice's book is one of the best ways to start.

Dee McCaffrey, CDC, author of *The Science of Skinny: Start Understanding Your Body's Chemistry and Stop Dieting Forever*

Table of Contents

Introduction

Like many mornings, I am standing in my kitchen thinking
about food. I have some organic, non GMO chicken thighs
cooking on the stove attempting to *again* make shredded chicken
with Mexican spice to go with my home made tortillas and
trimmings for the next few meals. I started this meal process
yesterday in the middle of hanging, taping and mudding drywall
in our guest bathroom. Losing track of the food on the stove, I
couldn't figure out why I smelled something burning until it hit
me. With many expletives and self-deprecating thoughts about
food and money waste, I ran to the kitchen with drywall mud on
my hands to find I had not turned the stove *off* 15 minutes earlier
but had turned it to high! Lucky for me my yogic training has
helped me to let things go easier than I did over twenty years ago,
so I opened the doors to air out the house and got back to dry
walling the bathroom.

It is this same yogic training and a daily meditation that
has kept me from reaching my boiling point with regard to the
food in our country. The fact that my husband and I share five
children, fourteen grandchildren and three great grandchildren
is what brought me to write this book. You see, I've been kind of
a health nut for about half my life and paid what I thought was
close attention to what I've been eating. Although I am still very

healthy, I have become painfully aware of many of the negative results of my loved ones consuming processed and GMO foods for much of their lives. This book tells many stories about those negative results and the dis-eases that follow. No doubt, you will find similarities in your life story and will, I hope, relate with compassion for all who are going through life unaware of the absolute degradation of our food "system".

This book is a direct result of my passion to share health with as many people as possible, shining a glaring spotlight on the division of wealth and health in our country and the world in general as it relates to food. My ultimate desire in sharing this information with you is that some of you will make better food choices for yourselves and your loved ones, resulting in a kinder, more compassionate outlook for the future of our species and planet.

Let me begin by saying that the bulk of information shared in this book is not new. Most of it has been available for more than twenty years. I highly recommend that if you are truly interested in eating healthier food and nourishing your body and those you love, that you educate yourself as I have by checking out the knowledgeable authors quoted throughout and listed in the "sources" section of this book.

In deciding on a title for my book, I wanted to keep it simple. It is my feeling that our creator, however you perceive that in your reality, made our food choices perfectly. All we had to do as guardians of this planet was learn to grow, love and care for, prepare and consume them to keep our bodies nourished and maintain stability in the soil and environment as a whole. Human's egotistic desire to change our foods and how they are grown to enhance their own lives and *lifestyles* over the last 60 to 70 years has brought us to the point in time that requires us to read every single label in our shopping basket and pantry before preparing a meal. We essentially live in fear of what we buy at the stores to feed our families and ourselves. Hence **"God Made Organics, not GMOs"** became my title, subtitled **"WTF's in Food Today?"** I am appalled at what manufacturers and growers are allowed to put in our foods, and after reading this book, I hope you are too. It is interesting to note that 50 to 60 years ago we didn't require the use of the word *organic* to describe our foods, they just were. When looking at the actual **matter** (substance or material) in our food, the more I learn, the more outraged I become ... and then I meditate.

By now you have probably heard about GMOs (genetically modified organisms) and how they are destroying our bodies, minds, spirits, the earth and its atmosphere in general. On the other hand, maybe you haven't! Either way, this book shares simple truths relative to our food sources, some stories of people already recovered or recovering from near death food related experiences and case studies from MD's, PHD.s, an NMD (naturopath), homeopaths, neuro science and everyday people. When conducting the interviews, I asked the interviewees or professionals a set of basic questions. Some of the questions were changed according to the area of expertise of the individual. I have not included *my voice* in asking the questions, but rather the answers of the individuals. I have however, listed the basic questions for your reference in the back of this book.

The purpose of this book is to scare the $#!T out of people to the extent that they may want to take a closer look at what they're ingesting and why they're not operating to their fullest capabilities. I'm simply sharing the information in a way that I hope will resonate with those who are still on the fence about our food sources. WAKE UP AND SMELL YOUR DIS-EASE! When I refer to 'dis ease', I want to emphasize that when we are not healthy, we are in a state of dis ease.

noun dis·ease \di- ˈ zēz\

: an illness that affects a person, animal, or plant : a condition that prevents the body or mind from working normally

: a problem that a person, group, organization, or society has and cannot stop

During a coffee meeting with a friend, we spoke of the fact that our food sources are deplorable and I shared with her that out of our fourteen grandchildren, seven have been diagnosed with one of the common acronyms of ADD, ADHD, OCD or depression. We are both of the understanding that these disabilities are largely due to the introduction of processed foods and *glyphosate* (more on this later) and the consequent lack of nutrition in utero, and are completely preventable given an education about where our agriculture has gone wrong and how to feed ourselves and our families whole, nutritious foods.

I was moved by her tale of terror during the ordeals of nearly losing her only son through consuming E-coli tainted spinach. [More about this in the chapter 2 interview with Juliana Goswick.]

Shortly after that meeting, I visited with my cousin who for 35 years has fostered special needs children with downs syndrome and autism among other diagnoses, or who were deposited in "the system" by the courts after their own special needs or drug-addled parent/s had abandoned them. I have always had a special place in my heart for her and her ability to love these children unconditionally as they go through lives very different from those of us who are considered "normal". While visiting, I noted that much of their foods are processed and full of sugar, salt, corn syrup and everything else that comes with the bulk of processed foods available in the supermarkets today. When I told her I was writing a book about food and nutrition, she was elated and really wanted to know more.

I am constantly amazed at the lack of understanding about how our life and food choices affect us and our offspring on a cellular level in some of the most basic, fundamental ways. I repeatedly hear from friends about food related maladies and those of their family.

Dr. Stephanie Seneff goes into more detail on the relationship of glyphosate to ADD, ADHD, Autism and other diseases in chapter 3.

My family and friends will attest that I have bothered, badgered and bugged them to no end about eating healthy, organic foods. Some have listened and some have not. For those who continue ingesting GMOs out of a lack of understanding of genetically modified "foods," I can only watch with compassion and sadness as the negative symptoms present themselves, and they do.

I believe that everyone on the planet has a gift unique to them, some simple, some more complex. It is our responsibility to share those gifts in a way that contributes to the well-being of all. We are all just playing a small part in a big orchestra. While I don't profess to have the knowledge of many of the people I have interviewed and quoted, I do have the ability and desire to assimilate and disseminate information. I feel especially compelled to share with others that which assists us in healing. That includes teaching art classes, yoga classes and meditation, and writing a book on the current food situation.

Also shared in this book is a list of foods that you should never eat and how to recognize healthy, non-GMO food in your store.

You picked this book up for a reason and I can only hope that it has to do with wanting to educate yourself further about how to recognize real food and become a healthier, happier person. Also included is a list of books and movies that I highly recommend for further education.

Chapter 1

· ·

Why Our Food Was Better In the 1940's Than It Is Now

In the 1940's, we still had real farms and farmers growing our fruits and vegetables, on fields that were crop rotated according to the best practices known to man over millennia. Those foods were, for the most part, pesticide free and full of nutrition. Our meats were raised on ranches, fields and farms according to what the animals were known to eat to be at their optimum health. These practices have proven to provide the best health for the animal and the consumer for thousands of years. Why did this change?

The fast food restaurants that originated in the 40's did NOT have the consumers' interests at heart when buying, preparing and selling food for consumption. As far as I can tell from the over-processed foods they used (and still use) in their restaurants, they didn't even honor the basic premise of plants and animals as sacred things, to be respected, valued and appreciated for what they provide the human species. From my research, they didn't place a whole lot of value on humankind either, unless it pertained to their own needs or desires for a better bottom line. They brought the factory system to their restaurants, firing all of the carhops, eliminating most of the menu items, and streamlining their restaurants to put out the cheapest food for the biggest volume. Each employee was trained to do one job, repeatedly all day long. That way, they could pay a lower wage, and when employees found they could not live on their wages and quit, they were easily replaced. This fast food model has become the template for fast food chains the world over.

Blind Trust

In "The Unsettling of America", Wendell Berry wrote:

> "The people will eat what the corporations decide for them to eat. They will be detached and removed from the sources of their life, joined to them only by corporate tolerance. They will have become consumer's-purely consumptive machines-which is to say, the slaves of producers. What these model farms very powerfully suggest, then, is that the concept of total control may be impossible to confine within the boundaries of the specialist enterprise-that it is impossible to mechanize production without mechanizing consumption, impossible to make machines of the soil, plants, and animals without making machines of people.
>
> To damage the earth is to damage your children. To despise the ground is to despise its fruit; to despise the fruit is to despise its eaters. The wholeness of health is broken by despite." (1)

What exactly is a GMO (Genetically Modified Organism)? In Genetic Roulette, Jeffrey M. Smith, Founder, Institute for Responsible Technology tells us:

*"It is when a gene from one species is forcibly injected in
the gene of another species. They can mix and match between
species that have never normally mated...*

*They have put spider genes into goats, hoping that
they can milk the goat and get spider web protein to make
bulletproof vests. They have inserted cow genes into pigs so
that the pigs would have cowhide. They have inserted human
genes into corn in the hopes to make spermicide".* (2)

There are two main categories of GMO crops, relative to
the food we eat. They are; Herbicide tolerant crops and pesticide
producing crops. The herbicide tolerant crops are designed so that
they can be sprayed and not die from the herbicide. The pesticide
producing crops are designed so that they produce their own
toxic insecticide. If a bug bites those plants, it breaks open their
stomach and kills them. Scientists are totally interchanging genes
between the normal species barriers, creating new organisms.
These new organisms were and are not part of the evolutionary
process. In Super-pigs and Wonder-corn, Dr. Michael W. Fox tells
us;

*"The U.S. Department of Agriculture (USDA) has
used public funds to apply this same technique [Transgenic
Animals, authors note] of inserting human genes into
animals to try to create giant pigs and sheep. Of the USDA's
"super-pigs" that carry the human growth gene, only one
in every 200 embryos survived. And those pigs that lived to
maturity had impaired vision, were arthritic and lethargic,*

and were prone to pneumonia because their immune systems were dysfunctional.

One female pig was born without an anus OR a vagina. Many others were too lethargic to stand. Other afflictions included enlarged hearts, ulcers, dermatitis and kidney disease." (3)

Although we have been told by the media *against* GMOs that the UK is virtually free of genetically modified foods:

"...several large UK grocery chains are already selling chickens that have been reared on GM feed produced from GM soya made by Monsanto. Worse still, they will not even label this meat as 'GM fed'.

The move by most retailers towards an embrace of GM foods represents something serious as it undermines consumer choice. Without proper labeling, shoppers cannot avoid eating GMO-fed animals.

It also opens the way to the domination of the food industry by biotech companies. Chicken feed is just the start. Once that precedent is established, the big firms will move on to all other types of livestock, in the process building a monopoly over feed supplies, as natural feed suppliers are forced out of business. This will make a mockery of the claim that GM technology will lead to lower prices. Once a monopoly or a cartel is created, there will be no real competition. We [author's emphasis] will all be at the mercy of the GM stranglehold. Such a situation could have disastrous consequences. For all the blithe rhetoric from the

*GM evangelists, we simply do not know what damage this
technology could cause to our bodies or to the environment.*

*The move by most retailers towards an embrace of GM
foods represents something serious as it undermines consumer
choice. Without proper labeling, shoppers cannot avoid
eating GMO-fed animals.*

*It also opens the way to the domination of the food
industry by biotech companies. Chicken feed is just the start.
Once that precedent is established, the big firms will move
on to all other types of livestock, in the process building
a monopoly over feed supplies, as natural feed suppliers
are forced out of business. This will make a mockery of
the claim that GM technology will lead to lower prices.
Once a monopoly or a cartel is created, there will be no
real competition. We [author's emphasis] will all be at the
mercy of the GM stranglehold. Such a situation could have
disastrous consequences. For all the blithe rhetoric from the
GM evangelists, we simply do not know what damage this
technology could cause to our bodies or to the environment."*
(4)

According to the Food Inc. documentary by Director Robert
Kenner, McDonald's is the largest purchaser of ground beef and
potatoes in the United States and one of the largest buyers of
pork, chicken, tomatoes, lettuce, and apples. When one buyer
has this much buying leverage on the food industry, some basic
inequities arise. From 25 percent in the 1970's to over 80 percent
today, the top-five food corporations' control of the beef industry
has grown to an alarmingly disproportionate dominance. That

gives them the power, via elected officials and buying authority, to control how our food is grown. In addition, it's not just *fast* food that is impacted. This has trickled down to the every-day food in local grocery stores. Out of an average of nearly 50,000 grocery foods in chain stores, over 90 percent has genetically modified ingredients in it. This has been done to make food less perishable, to produce it faster, and to make it cheaper, and in larger quantities than Americans can consume. These corporations claim to want to feed the masses, but what they offer should not be considered *real food* as it was known more than 70 years ago.

You might ask yourself, how does this kind of dominance happen in a free country? We the people allow it by spending our hard-earned cash to feed our families in what we have been led to believe is the cheapest way possible. However, as I will establish in this book, those cheap, fast and modified foods come at a real health cost, maybe not today, after your first hamburger or rib sandwich, or even one year from now but definitely over time. You vote with your dollars.

Low Income Families and Nutrition

Dr. Michael W. Fox tells us:

> *"Even the public's health and the rights of consumers to wholesome food, clean air, and clean water are sacrificed. In order to preserve the status quo of economic determinism, new medical and legislative fixes are found to correct these residual problems rather than change values and practices to correct the underlying problem. For example, applying poisonous pesticides and other agrichemicals is profitable, as are the medical procedures necessary to treat cancer, birth*

defects, sterility, and other diseases linked with agripoisons. Preventative medicine is as unprofitable to the medical industry as organic farming is to agribusiness – but certainly not to the consuming populace. It is disturbing to contemplate the irony of applying genetic engineering technology to correct a host of human health problems that are due in part to the misapplication of chemical and medical technologies in agriculture and farm animal production. Genetic engineering in human medicine is not really progressive because its primary focus is not preventative; it is essentially yet another profitable, alternative, interventive technological fix, the primary beneficiaries of which will be investors, manufacturers, hospitals, and medical administrators – not the public". (5)

Are you really going to trust your health and that of your family to corporations whose sole interest is a good bottom line? People will use a hand towel to open a public bathroom door to avoid germs, but they will carelessly toss processed, GM foods laced with harmful chemicals into their grocery carts. With all the safety laws in our country about seat belts, metal slides and other playground equipment considered dangerous, safety locks on the cupboards and doors, shouldn't we consider the possibility that our bodies require the same attention to safety, compassion, and awareness? If not now, then when? We must understand the real and present dangers facing us today in our once sacred food supply.

We seem to be chasing our tails trying to figure out what to do first? Do we eat real food or try to find real health? Moreover, which should come first? If we could find and eat real, nutrient rich food that contained all the amino acids, minerals, and trace minerals that were in our farmers' fields 80 years ago, we would have healthier brain and body cells. Healthier bodies and minds would result in fewer occurrences of diabetes in children and adults; fewer diagnoses of ADD, ADHD, OCD, less Autism (yes, recent science is linking Autism to GMOs and a lack of nutrition in utero), fewer thyroid problems, less heart disease and the list goes on. Consider the statistics in our country of low-income families. From FRAC, Food Research and Action Center:

"Due to the additional risk factors associated with poverty, food insecure and low-income people are especially vulnerable to obesity. More specifically, obesity among food insecure people – as well as among low-income people – occurs in part because they are subject to the same influences as other Americans (e.g., more sedentary lifestyles, increased portion sizes), but also because they face unique challenges in adopting healthful behaviors as described below.

• Limited resources and lack of access to healthy, affordable foods.

• Low-income neighborhoods frequently lack full-service grocery stores and farmers' markets where residents can buy a variety of fruits, vegetables, whole grains, and low-fat dairy products.

Instead, residents – especially those without reliable transportation – may be limited to shopping at small neighborhood convenience and corner stores, where fresh produce and low-fat items are limited, if available at all. One of the most comprehensive reviews of U.S. Studies examining neighborhood disparities in food access found that neighborhood residents with better access to supermarkets and limited access to convenience stores tend to have healthier diets and reduced risk for obesity.

When available, healthy food is often more expensive, whereas refined grains, added sugars, and fats are generally inexpensive and readily available in low-income communities. Households with limited resources to buy enough food often try to stretch their food budgets by purchasing cheap, energy-dense foods that are filling – that is, they try to maximize their calories per dollar in order to stave off hunger. While less expensive, energy-dense foods typically have lower nutritional quality and, because of overconsumption of calories, have been linked to obesity.

When available, healthy food – especially fresh produce – is often of poorer quality in lower income neighborhoods, which diminishes the appeal of these items to buyers.

Low-income communities have greater availability of fast food restaurants, especially near schools. These restaurants serve many energy-dense, nutrient-poor foods at relatively low prices. Fast food consumption is associated with a diet high in calories and low in nutrients, and frequent consumption may lead to weight gain." (6)

People are lulled into thinking that they can't afford organic whole foods and should be spending their hard-earned incomes on cheap, processed, and fast foods. They are manipulated by media hype and false advertising into the "American way" of consumerism at its worst, buying *socially acceptable* trinkets to entertain them while spending their free time on the couch, watching meaningless reality TV, degrading news stories highlighting everything that's wrong about people, our country and our world, and eating the very products that brought them to this beleaguered state to begin with.

If I understand the science of Dr. Seneff in Chapter two correctly, if we continue to consume the non-foods that we find in our major grocery stores, and many of the health-food chains, we will never have the brain capacity to discern why we feel like crap, have no energy, are irritable, can't hold down a job, and can't hold our attention or that of our children for more than a nanosecond. It's no wonder we don't understand why we're unable to lose that extra 10 to 110 pounds!

When speaking about obesity in our country my Chiropractor, Dr. Heidi Hartman-Taylor succinctly stated:

"It's not their fault. My ex-husband had a car-wreck and had major surgeries on his neck. After the surgeries he developed sleep apnea and had a blood sugar problem. Prior to the accident, he lived on Atkins, eating a low-carbohydrate diet of about 60 grams a day. He never cared about sugar. After the accident, he went from six feet tall, 180 pounds to 300/310 pounds. He couldn't breathe or stop eating sugar".

It was Heidi's belief that her husband's obesity was primarily brought on by the drugs he was given after surgery along with his new addiction to refined sugar.

We are given false hopes for nutritious, fast, inexpensive foods for families with two working parents who don't have the time or energy to prepare meals. Even when a parent makes the effort to buy fresh fruits, vegetables and proteins, they are not getting the nutrition they were promised because of the lack of minerals and trace minerals in the soil (unless they buy organic). The endless spiral continues until disease rears its ugly head and one or more family members' gets seriously sick and requires medical intervention. Now you are down to one parent working two jobs in order to supplement the others need to stay home sick or with a sick child. Medical costs soar and divorce is common due to the stress.

Nutrient Deficient Soil

Dr. John Gray, Ph.D. states in his book published in 2003, The Mars & Venus Diet & Exercise Solution:

> *"Our cells are starving and our brains are not producing healthy brain chemistry because the foods we eat are deficient in minerals. No matter how well you select the right foods for yourself, it will not be satisfying and you will want to overeat. This is so because everything you buy from the produce department of your grocery store is deficient in trace minerals."* (7)

The people in our country are not intentionally dumbing down; their brains simply are not being nourished on a cellular level because they've been trusting their food sources. They no longer have the brainpower to *think* healthy and make better choices. They are in a self-induced coma of blind, anesthetized complacency. Dr. Gray further states that:

> *"Organic food products have a higher mineral content, but the level of these minerals is not even close to what it used*

*to be just 50 years ago", (Now over 70, author's note). Even
with plenty of water, we can't get what we need, because the
fresh produce is mineral-deficient. Almost all of the processed
food is stripped of its natural mineral content."*

Dr. Linus Pauling, twice the winner of a Nobel Prize, said:
*"You can trace every sickness, every disease, and every
ailment to a mineral deficiency." (8)*

Most of the problems we suffer today began with the
mineral-deficient land our food is grown on and the animals
that eat those grains and produce. The minerals that are the
fundamental building blocks to life are virtually gone from our
soils, and consequently our food sources. The level of iron, a vital
mineral for good health, has dropped 55 percent in the average
rump steak. During the same period magnesium plummeted by 21
percent and calcium was significantly lower. In fact every mineral
except the three used to fertilize today's farmlands, is anywhere
from 10 percent to 40 percent lower than 60 years ago.

If the chicken came first, what did it eat before it laid eggs?
If the egg came first, what were the nutrients it fed on before
becoming a chicken? These days our chickens are fed GMO feed,
while made to stand on legs too weak to hold the weight of the
huge breasts they are *designed* to grow by being injected with
growth hormones as little chicks. The eggs that come from today's
factory farmed laying hens are composed of the same nutrient
deficient biomass.

<u>Dana Murdoch Interview on CAFO's</u>

My friend Dana Murduck, a former private practice rehabilitation counselor was frequently called from the human resource department of the Alaskan Pipeline to do testing of the workers who were injured on the job. She states that:

> *"Out of six workers, at least two of them couldn't read, many of them in their 30's and 40's, being skilled iron, construction or physical workers. They were not dumb but they could not read. Many had dyslexia, ADD or ADHD and most had actually graduated from high school."*

In that same professional capacity she was later called by the Human Resources Dept. of Zackey Farms to look into on the job injuries. She was hired to find out what the physical requirements of the injured party's jobs were so that the doctor could then determine if the person could return to work after their injury. As Dana observed:

> *"The HR person out at Zackey Farms, for some reason really liked me. I don't understand it (laughs). It was like punishment! I knew not to eat anything before I went because I was going to throw up. You'd smell it right as you got to the gate. The first thing you'd do is drive through this deep concrete depression filled with antibiotics and all kinds of disinfectant chemicals that would go around your wheels and car to disinfect the undercarriage. As soon as you get there, you'd have to*

put on a hazmat (hazardous materials) suit with eye protection and mask before going into this hell!

When I grew up we raised chickens in a coop the old-fashioned way. The chickens were allowed to walk in the yard, scratching and pecking under the sun, laying their eggs in the coop. Occasionally a weasel or an owl would break in and kill a chicken. That was the worst thing that would ever happen. It didn't smell great but it never made me throw up! The little chicks would come in the mail and we had a big cardboard box out on the porch with a heat lamp over it. As many as 100 eggs would stay there for a while. Of course, not all of them survived or hatched but we probably had more than fifty chickens most of the time.

So I go out to the processing plant and as you walk in there is this chain kind of conveyor that is going down the length of about two football fields. Live chickens were coming out of this chute and workers would take the chickens and hook them on a conveyer hook upside down, then down a little further they're eviscerated while still alive, all the intestines being pulled out. Then they are put into boiling water to be d-feathered. Then they're dipped into what the employees refer to as the 'fecal soup,' which was like a hot water bath full of feces, left over blood and everything that was still in or on the chicken. Then they would go to the processing line with band saws where they were sectioned (cut up). Then they'd go to a line where women would check them and remove or check this or that, then move on down the line. Depending on what they're packaging that day, the chicken would be packaged for delivery. The smell in the packaging area would be so unbelievably horrible. And Zackey Farms advertises all natural.

I would have to go to the Zackey Farms California plant often because of the nature of repetitive work on those disassembly lines where people do one thing, repeatedly, wearing out and getting hurt. I would have to describe the lifting, carrying, pushing, pulling, and the number of times per minute they would have to do something, or what kind of force was required to do a particular job. I had an instrument for pushing and pulling that would calibrate the poundage. It was like working in hell! Absolute hell!

Then they had the chicks that went to the hatchery. I thought, well this will be better right? You drive again through another concrete pit, because these chickens are so sensitive to any kind of disease, that anything will wipe them all out (*CAFO farms) because they have no immune system.

The third place I went to was where they have the laying hens. That was relatively humane. Again I had to go through the 'ditch' to these long, long buildings they call 'ranges'. They call them ranges so they can say they are 'free range' chickens because they're not chained down. Inside the range I was amazed that the chickens actually were able to move around a little bit. They could jump down and walk around on the floor. They had laying boxes and it was not that different from fifty or sixty years ago. The layers were allowed to live for a year because that is the most productive length of time for laying hens. They were allowed to have a 'chicken-ish life'. They never got out into the sun or into a *yard. There were skylights but they were pretty much in the dark for all their lives. Then they become roasting chickens.*

It is my understanding that the eggs we buy in the store are extremely old. They've been in cold storage for sometimes up to a year, which is why the yolks lie flat and don't stand up like the eggs you'd get straight from the farmers market for $5.00 a dozen. They are worth it because they taste like eggs and there are no chemical surprises in them.

Chickens are supposed to be able to go into a yard to scratch and peck for pebbles to clean their gullets for digestion. They are also social animals that would normally have a 'pecking order' among the flock. None of that is available to them in these industrial chicken farms. They used to be fed ground up dead chickens and all kinds of other stuff but I think there are regulations now, particularly in California, that chickens cannot be raised as cannibals. Now they're fed mostly millet based and GMO grains. In this country, you can't buy any grains in quantity that aren't GMO. For our distillery (Thumb Butte Distillery) (9) we have to buy our grains from France, Italy and Poland!

OK. Now we have to talk about the chicks. That was the most horrible day. It was close to Easter and I had images of these cute, furry little chicks in my mind. What I saw was huge conveyer lines coming down from an upper level, holding trays with eggs in them. Somehow, they're able to control when every egg in these boxes hatch. Right then, the eggs are all cracking, and these little fluff balls are coming out. It's like a miracle that all of these eggs are hatching at the same time! Then there is a big table like a stainless steel lazy Susan shallow dish, and in the middle, it has another lazy Susan thing going around with needles coming out of it. It's most likely fed from below with the antibiotics, steroids and breast hormones. The chicks come out and are grabbed by the workers. If one falls on the ground, it's kicked out of the way. That really bothered me because all the corners are filled with dead chicks. The workers grab them and put them on the needles, knowing which needles to put the chicks on. Then their beaks are clipped off, and their feet were trimmed down to virtually nothing. Then they would go off on another conveyer belt to their cages for sixty days where they're fed a diet of mostly liquid slurry full of stuff that makes them grow big, white breasts."

Dr. Mercola On CAFO's

With regard to CAFO (concentrated animal feeding operations) Dr. Mercola writes:

"Sickness is the norm for animals raised in these CAFOs—the large-scale factory farms on which 99 percent of American chickens come from. These animals are also typically fed genetically engineered (GE) corn and soybeans, which is a far cry from their natural diet of seeds, green plants, insects, and worms. This unnatural diet further exacerbates disease promulgation. Processing byproducts such as chicken feathers and other animal parts can also be added to the feed.

To prevent the inevitable spread of disease from stress, overcrowding, lack of vitamin D (as CAFO chickens may never see the light of day), and an unnatural diet, the animals are routinely fed antibiotics (hormones, on the other hand, are not permitted in American-raised chickens). Those antibiotics pose a direct threat to human health, and contaminate the environment when they run off into lakes, rivers, aquifers, and drinking water. According to a landmark "Antibiotic Resistance Threat Report" published by the CDC, two million Americans become infected with antibiotic-resistant bacteria each year, and at least 23,000 of them die as a direct result of those infections. Research suggests you have a 50/50 chance of buying meat tainted with drug-resistant bacteria when you buy it from your local grocery store. In some cases, the risk may be even greater."

Factory farmed chicken may be cheap, but the ultimate price you pay is high."(10)

"Ethical objections to the genetic engineering of birds and other animals have focused primarily on the violation of species integrity (Rifkin), although attention has also been given to the suffering of individual animals and to the definition of animals as patentable 'manufactures and compositions of matter'.

This definition represents a further debasement of nonhuman animals from their traditional low status as human property devoid of value and claims in their own right. Animals used for genetic engineering are not recognized as whole beings but only as technology components. The indifference to the animals who are being used in genetic engineering experiments was expressed by the researcher who told his colleagues at a poultry science meeting in 1992.

We are no longer selling broilers [i.e. baby 'meat-type' chickens], we are selling pieces. A knowledge of how broilers *of different strains and sexes grow and become pieces is increasingly important."* (11)

For years, we have been told that another great source of protein is soybeans. We're doing everything we can with tofu - soaking it, frying it, putting sauces on it, making ice cream and smoothies out of it, just to make it more palatable. Now we find that even tofu isn't as safe as we are led to believe! Even if the soy *is* grown in other countries, 90 percent of it is GMO. Eighty-five percent of all corn grown in the United States is genetically modified. There are 420 million acres (and growing!) of GMOs worldwide. The world demand for pesticides will soon reach $52 BILLION! Where do you think those pesticides wind up? That's right, in the very cellular structures of the food *AND WATER* that these "food corporations" claim will feed the world. That's what scares me and should scare you!

More than 80 years ago, around the 1930's, our government issued a report acknowledging that farming systems in the U.S. have stripped our soil of minerals, leaving our food mineral-deficient. This information was the precursor to the health supplement industry. Millions upon millions of dollars annually are spent on supplementing our food in an effort to get and stay healthy. Foods that used to carry all of the nutrition we need are virtually gone with the exception of a few organically farmed foods. Now, many of those have been tainted with cross drifting of pollens and seeds from GMO farm conglomerates, traveling with the winds, birds and bugs to what started as organic farms close by.

> *"GMO seeds are patented. Between 1997 and 2010, the*
> *owners of those seeds (mainly Monsanto) filed more than*
> *144 patent-infringement lawsuits against farmers, and won*
> *judgments saying that they made use of the seed without*
> *paying the requisite royalties." (12)*

If that doesn't tick you off, add to the equation that:

> *"Monsanto has developed a reputation for zealously*
> *defending patents on its genetically altered crops, which*
> *include the patented "Roundup Ready" soybeans, corn*
> *and cotton, genetically altered to tolerate treatments of its*
> *Roundup weed killer." (12)*

> *"In the 20th century, many farmers learned that they*
> *didn't have to add the compost to the soil that contained over*
> *77 minerals and trace minerals, instead they used artificial*
> *fertilizers with only about three nutrients (minerals and trace*
> *minerals). These few nutrients made the fruits and vegetables*
> *look and taste almost the same as crops grown with the*
> *original soil components. These farmers were encouraged by*
> *corporations to use their pesticides and GMO seeds, reducing*
> *the weeds and bugs and changing their basic farming*
> *techniques. They bypassed the process of adding mineral-*
> *rich compost to their soil that allowed plants to thrive on the*
> *nitrates and minerals needed to grow." (7)*

The result of this carnage of the soil is mineral deficient
plants and soil. The soil is no longer replenished with those 77
minerals and trace minerals and ultimately it is stripped and
our food is empty of nutrition. Today, we cannot physically eat

enough fruits and vegetables to get the minerals our bodies need to thrive without supplements and eating organic, non-GMO foods. I'll talk more about this in chapter three. Frederick Douglass wrote in 1857:

> "If there is no struggle there is no progress. Those who profess to favor freedom and yet deprecate agitation are men who want to crop without plowing the ground; they want the rain without thunder and lightning. They want the ocean without the awful roar of its many waters...power concedes nothing without a demand. It never did and it never will. Find out just what any people will quietly submit to and you have found out the exact measure of injustice and wrong, which will be imposed upon them. The limits of tyrants are prescribed by the endurance of those whom they oppress." (13)

Our food has changed more drastically in the last 70 years than in the last 10,000!

Chapter 2

· ·

What's OK About the Degradation of Our Food?

Nothing! It was grown correctly from the beginning but all of our meddling has made today's food unrecognizable to our bodies.

Why would anyone believe that they have a better way than our creator intended to grow our precious food sources? This is EGO at its worst. Deepak Chopra says EGO stands for "Edging God Out". This has a resounding parallel to a mindset of fixing something that isn't broken in order to make millions.

Interview With Juliana Goswick

My friend Juliana Goswick was kind enough to share her story of terror surrounding her then seven-year young son Jacob's near death experience with E.coli poisoning. He was the first diagnosed case in Arizona, having consumed tainted spinach the week of August 21, 2006. As we sat in a restaurant, she showed me the scrapbook she had made for him saying, "I felt it was important to give this to him as a gift, because this was the paperwork they gave him at Children's hospital to explain how his kidneys work, so that he could understand what was happening in his body".

[Juliana Goswick] *"Everything bad that could happen did. The doctor was great as he told us what could happen, and everything he said could happen, did. I would ask the Doctor, 'Is he going to make it through today? Tell me!'*

Jacob was in the Children's Hospital of Phoenix for close to two months, and, shocking, he still made straight a's that year.

The tainted spinach leaves were found to have come from a California farm, whose produce went to Wisconsin and Arizona, along with 24 other states. There was a cattle fill close by, where the cattle were being force fed grain, while acid resistant E.coli developed in their gut. They defecate in the rainwater running right down into the field next to it, which was an organic spinach field. People think they can wash the leaf and will be fine. That is not how the E.coli bacteria grows. It starts in the earth and flows through the root system of the plant. It can't be washed off. You have to protect the soil and the parameters of what's planted around your crops. That's why I have such respect for the organic farmer. So many of my friends say, 'I don't buy organic foods, they're too expensive.' It's expensive because they give up part of their land that they could plant on to create Hedgerows*. But that's not enough. They need to look at whether there are pigs, wild boar, or cattle nearby. And the other issue is why are we force feeding grain to cattle? We need to go back to slow food and the natural way of producing cattle.

The relationship between the consumer and the farmer needs to be examined. I had great trust in them, but I don't anymore. Jacob still to this day will not eat spinach unless it's locally grown. That to me is really the only safe way to get good food. And it's interesting because the government wants to put fees and restrictions on the small farmer, but if you look, all the cases of food poisoning and miss-handling of produce is factory farmed. So they (the government) slap these fees on small farmers that they can't afford, and they go out of business. So where does that leave us? The relationship between the consumer and the farmer needs to be respected and trusted and it also needs to be questioned because everything is in their hands. It's a profession that needs to be revered and I don't think it is anymore.

There were 129 cases of E.coli poisoning across the US from this outbreak alone. A two year old died in Salt Lake City as a direct result of E.coli tainted food.

Jacob was a kid who loved Popeye and wanted to emulate him by eating spinach. I remember the night at dinner that Jacob went in that fridge and made himself more salad. Jacob was a kid that when he would make a connection in a restaurant and the server wanted to be nice and offer to treat him to dessert, he would ask them for more salad. He wouldn't go for the dessert."

After Jacob's ordeal was over, the family decided they wanted to get the word out about food safety by speaking to the local Board of Supervisors and with a letter writing campaign to Senator John McCain. Here is the letter Jacob wrote:

Senator John McCain
241 Russell Senate Office Building
Washington D.C. 20510

4/27/09

Dear Senator McCain,

Two years ago when I was eight, I had E. coli. It was horrible. I'm flying from Prescott Arizona to Washington D.C. to make food safer for people. I don't want anyone to go through the experience that I did. After eating a spinach salad, I had a bad stomachache, and got sent to the hospital. I remember being in so much pain that I had to be transferred to a bigger hospital two hours away from home. I was on dialysis for four weeks and missed two months of school. I began having psychological fear of eating spinach and other foods. I used to be a really good swimmer until this happened. It took me a long time to recover and win ribbons again. Please help our food become safer by voting 'Yes' on H.R. 875. No one should get sick on something that should be healthy.

Sincerely,

Jacob Louis Goswick
Jacob Louis Goswick
600 Lee Blvd
Prescott AZ 86303

Food Safety Modernization Act

The House passed the Food Safety Bill by a vote of 215 to 144 giving the Food & Drug Administration greater authority over food products, whether they come from this country or are imported from abroad.

This bill gave the FDA the ability to set standards for growing and harvesting produce, aiming to reduce the likelihood of contamination in the fields.

Here are a few of the mandates from the bill:

 # 7 Risk/Hazard Prevention

"Food production facilities must alert the FDA, through writing, of all identified hazardous practices currently in place and their plans to implement preventive measures going forward." (14)

Isn't this the fox guarding the hen house? I wonder how many food corporations voluntarily report their hazardous practices to the FDA.

#9 Regulations on Food Unfit To Eat

"The FDA, along with the Department of Homeland Security and Department of Agriculture, will issue regulations that prevent food companies from knowingly including illegal additives, chemicals or other substances in their food products." (14)

This is one regulation that has gotten entirely lost in translation. What exactly is considered an illegal additive or chemical relative to long-term human consumption? How is this regulated?

#12 Inspection Frequencies

"Under the new law, the FDA must increase the
frequency of its inspections. High-risk food production
facilities will be inspected every three years while low-risk
facilities will be visited within seven years of the law's
passing. Each year the FDA must report to Congress the
frequency and cost of inspections." (14)

Wow! *Every three to seven years* the production company can
expect an inspection! Now doesn't that make you feel safe in the
years where no inspection is required?

"Proposition 37 in California was a bill proposed
to label GMOs which would require food made from any
genetically altered plant or animal material to be labeled by
the summer of 2014. The passing of this bill, which would
impact industry labeling practices across the country, was
shut down by Monsanto, DOW Agro Sciences, Dupont,
Bayer, Nestle, Con Agra, Pepsi and Coke with multi-million
dollar campaigns (by some accounts over one million dollars
per day) of miss-information to consumers. One of their own
commercials stated that:

"Some foods would need special labels to be sold in
California, while others would get special exemptions."(15)

These corporations further stated in their commercials:

"This illogical, unfair labeling proposition makes no
sense. And it would increase costs for California farmers and

food companies by over a billion dollars a year and increase grocery bills for a typical family by $400.00 per year." (15)

Really? Consumers in more than 50 other countries already have GMO labeling and not just on their own country's food but on products being imported from the US. What is wrong with that picture?

In the following article on pesticide use, we read that the bulk of pesticide use started with chemical defoliants, left over from the Malaysian and Vietnam wars.

Agent Orange

According to Wikipedia:

"Trioxone and the 2, 4, 5-T and 2, 4-D (Agent Orange), were primarily manufactured by ICI during the early 1950s. The British were the first to employ herbicides and defoliants to destroy the crops, bushes, and trees of communist insurgents in Malaya during the Malayan Emergency.

In mid-1961, President Ngo Dinh Diem of South Vietnam asked the United States to conduct aerial herbicide spraying in his country. In August of that year, the South Vietnamese Air Force initiated herbicide operations with American help. But Diem's request launched a policy debate in the White House and the State and Defense Departments. However, U.S. officials considered using it, pointing out that the British had already used herbicides and defoliants during the Malayan Emergency in the 1950s. In November 1961, President John F. Kennedy authorized the start of Operation

Ranch Hand, the codename for the U.S. Air Force's herbicide program in Vietnam.

Agent Orange was manufactured for the U.S. Department of Defense primarily by **Monsanto Corporation and Dow Chemical.** *It was given its name from the color of the orange-striped barrels in which it was shipped, and was by far the most widely used of the so-called 'Rainbow Herbicides.' The 2, 4, 5-T used to produce Agent Orange was contaminated with 2, 3, 7, 8-tetrachlorodibenzodioxin (TCDD), an extremely toxic dioxin compound. In some areas, TCDD concentrations in soil and water were hundreds of times greater than the levels considered safe by the U.S. Environmental Protection Agency.*

In the absence of specific customary or positive international humanitarian law regarding herbicidal warfare, a draft convention, prepared by a Working Group set up within the Conference of the Committee on Disarmament (CCD), was submitted to the UN General Assembly in 1976. In that same year, the First Committee of the General Assembly decided to send the text of the draft convention to the General Assembly, which adopted Resolution 31/72 on December 10, 1976, with the text of the Convention attached as an annex thereto. The convention, namely the Environmental Modification Convention, was opened for signature and ratification on May 18, 1977, and entered into force in October 5, 1978. The convention prohibits the military or other hostile use of environmental modification techniques having widespread, long-lasting or severe effects. Many states do not regard this as a complete ban on the use of herbicides and defoliants in warfare but it does require case-by-case consideration". (16)

In other words, it's unsafe in any of its applications. It was made that way for its intended use DURING WAR TIME! When we look back over the years at anything in our history that has caused pain and suffering for humankind, it can be traced to the desire for wealth beyond what is necessary for daily life on this planet.

Here is an interesting scenario:

- A mother gives birth to a child after she has been eating processed, GMO foods during her life and most importantly for this scenario, during her pregnancy.
- Due to a lack of essential minerals and trace minerals (among other nutrients) in their food, her child is born and grows up with behavioral problems diagnosed as ADD, ADHD, OCD or depression.
- The child also consumes processed, GMO foods during his or her life.
- Because of blind trust in our food sources, the parents do not understand the connection between ingesting these non-foods and their child's abnormalities.
- Due to the child's behavior, the school system mandates that the child be prescribed drugs such as Strattera (Atomoxetine HCL by Eli Lilly) for the problem or be removed from school.
- The child exhibits the "common side effects" of the drug listed for children including one or more of the symptoms of upset stomach, decreased appetite, nausea,

vomiting, tiredness, dizziness and mood swings (see Chapter 4 "Prescription Drug TV Ads").

- The child feels physically ill and abnormal, and is having difficulty learning because he or she is sick and gets sent home with regularity, thus falling further behind in school.
- The parents now have to leave work and are upset with the child for not being "normal".
- The child continues on the path of least resistance to find friends who are like them so they can feel acceptance.
- The child grows up without the ability to read, write, understand basic math principles, or problem solve. As a result, the child lacks the tools to find and keep work.
- The child finds drugs or alcohol to assuage their inner pain, and since they cannot keep any menial work, they steal, are caught, and enter the "justice" system.

So again, we experience how processed, GMO foods affect a chain of events that only those in the one percent can benefit from, and I'd be willing to wager that the majority of those people don't eat processed foods.

Who benefits?

- All the way back to the mother eating what she trusted was good food; **food and chemical industries,**
- The child eating the same foods; **food and chemical industries**
- The parents trusting the medical profession to help their child live a more normal life; **pharmaceutical and medical industry**

- The eventual repercussions of an ineffectual system, whether it be the Government prison system or **privately held prisons**. Rates of attention deficit hyperactivity disorder (ADHD) are remarkably high among prison inmates.
- Unemployment or general bad health; back to **food, chemical, medical and pharmaceutical industries**

Of course, this is only one possible scenario. I will present a few more further on in the book.

Big Salaries at Monsanto

Here is a list of salaries for Monsanto executives according to the 'Huffington Post', June 4, 2014:

Hugh Grant -

Chairman of the Board and Chief Executive Officer: $12,112,481

Brett D. Begemann -

President and Chief Operating Officer: $3,839,242

Robert T. Fraley, Ph.D. -

Executive Vice President and Chief Technology Officer: $3,703,324

Of Monsanto's 1.48 billion dollars in profits, there are many more grossly high executive salaries on the list, but this gives you a good idea of where the money goes. About half of these numbers are equity based and half are cash based." (17)

A quote from the 'New York Times, Business Day' – April 3, 2013:

"Monsanto, the world's largest seed company, raised its full-year profit forecast on Wednesday after reporting better-than-expected earnings in its second quarter, driven by strength in its global corn and herbicide businesses..."

Another:

"Still, some analysts were less enthusiastic about Monsanto's results than they might have been because the gains that beat their already high earnings expectations stemmed not from seed sales but from the company's smaller glyphosate herbicide business". (18)

I don't doubt for a minute that they are also at a much lower tax rate. Speaking of lower tax rates, Monsanto was in the news in 2014 when attempting to buy Syngenta, and then attempting to reincorporate as a Swiss corporation. This is a process known as corporate inversion, which would allow Monsanto to dramatically reduce the taxes it pays in the U.S.

The Roundup®/Glyphosate Connection

What is Glyphosate (glī-fo-sate)? An Article in Natural News explains glyphosate as follows:

"Monsanto's infamous Roundup contains the hotly debated compound called glyphosate. This merciless herbicide is also found in 750 or more U.S. products. An herbicide like this infiltrates the landscape and accumulates in mammals, especially bone, hindering cellular detoxification along the way.

A destroyer, glyphosate annihilates plants building blocks of life, tearing apart amino acids. By disrupting

*the "shikimate pathway" in plants and microorganisms,
glyphosate creeps inside leaves and stalk, raping natural
life processes. Glyphosate also destroys the beneficial
microorganism in the human gut, destroying the human
immune system.*

*Glyphosate's mere existence has led scientists to develop
Roundup-Ready seeds, which are genetically modified
to resist the glyphosate. This has allowed an up-rise in
engineered food, which the human body cannot naturally
process. Farmers can now plant the genetically engineered
crop and spray their fields simultaneously with glyphosate.
Weeds are expected to die and terminator crops are
engineered to withstand the chemicals. This has led to global
food dominance by corporations like Monsanto, who push
their genetically altered food onto Third World countries all
under the guise of 'feeding world hunger.' Now farmers feel
that they must depend on these chemical companies for seed,
and are cornered into using herbicides like glyphosate to have
a more productive crop.*

*The human body was intended to eat unmodified,
natural food. Chemical-laced genetically engineered science
has manufactured a new-age frontier of food that is wiping
out small organic farmers from the picture. As science
takes a short cut and eradicates the fields, it globalizes food
production. Small organic farmers who work hard to protect
the balance of the ecosystem and purity of food, have felt
the squeeze global chemical companies are putting on their
ability to provide whole food." (19)*

In "The Horrific Truth about Roundup" an Interview by Dr. Jeffrey Smith of Dr. Stephanie Seneff, Dr. Seneff states:

> "As of March of 2015, one in fifty children will be diagnosed with autism. At the current rate of autism spectrum diagnoses, in twenty years every other child will have autism". (20)

Government Corruption

In the film Genetic Roulette, Jeffrey Smith states:

> "Because of the heavy spraying of Roundup, in the Midwest 60 to 100 percent of the air samples, water samples, rain samples and surface water samples have tested positive for glyphosate. It is found in the blood of pregnant women and their fetuses. It has been found in the urine of city dwellers in Germany. It is omnipresent!
>
> The overwhelming consensus among the scientists working at the FDA was not only that GMOs were different, but that they were dangerous. They could lead to allergies, toxins, new diseases and nutritional problems they said repeatedly in their memos. They urged their superiors to require long-term studies but were ignored. Why? The person in charge of policy at the FDA was Michael Taylor, Monsanto's former attorney, later Monsanto's Vice President; now back at the FDA as U.S. Food Safety Czar. The FDA does not approve any genetically modified crops. There is a voluntary consultation process, where companies like Monsanto can produce whatever science it wants. If the FDA asks for further information, they are typically ignored. At the end of this meaningless exercise, the FDA produces a

*letter, which reminds Monsanto that it is its responsibility to
determine that the foods are safe..."* (21)

This is again a scenario where the fox is guarding the hen
house-a former Monsanto employee working at the FDA.

Three more examples of seemingly incestuous relationships
and why nothing is being done to keep our food safe at the
Government level are:

Michael Taylor, served five years as an FDA attorney, then
worked for Monsanto as a private practice attorney (King and
Spalding Law Firm) for Monsanto, then returned to the FDA in
the capacity of Deputy Commissioner for Policy to oversee GMO
foods. After Monsanto got from him what they needed in that
capacity, he was promoted to Vice President of Public Policy. In
2009 he returned to the FDA as the senior advisor of food safety.
In 2010 he became Deputy Commissioner for Foods, a position
created specifically for him. (22)

Tom Vilsack, leading GMO advocate, Governor of the
year 2001, Biotechnology Industry Association. US Secretary of
Agriculture 2009. (22.a)

Roger Beachy, Director, Danforth Center, Monsanto.
Director USDA NIFA 2009. (22b.)

*"Since the 1990s, Americans have been consuming foods
that should not have been on the market until proven safe. In
addition our own FDA scientists told the FDA that they were
not safe from the beginning."* (57)

"A French court found Monsanto guilty of lying;
falsely advertising its Roundup herbicide as 'biodegradable,'
'environmentally friendly,' and claiming it 'left the soil clean.'

Mounting evidence now tells us just how false such
statements are. 'I don't believe that Monsanto is one of the
most evil companies on the planet for nothing. The company
has done absolutely nothing to improve their worldwide
influence on human and environmental health...' (23)

In the video interview with Dr. Seneff, Jeffrey Smith says:

"Monsanto, during some reflective moment, must have
asked, 'What would Darth Vader do?' Because what they've
come up with is a way of pretending that they're beneficial
and then insinuating themselves into the food and agriculture
industry, and now it turns out that what they have is very,
very dangerous..." (20)

The Horrific Truth About Roundup Report

The following report (found on Mercola.com) is included in
its entirety to share just how harmful glyphosate really is.
Although much of the article is a bit difficult to decipher in my
limited scientific knowledge and possibly yours, please note the
highlighted areas in particular. From these you will get the gist of
the information needed to come to your own conclusion or in fact,
do further research on your own.

"A new peer-reviewed report authored by Anthony
Samsel, a retired science consultant, and a long time
contributor to the Mercola.com Vital Votes Forum, and Dr.
Stephanie Seneff, a research scientist at the Massachusetts

Institute of Technology (MIT), reveals how glyphosate wrecks human health.

In the interview above, Dr. Seneff summarizes the two key problems caused by glyphosate in the diet: nutritional deficiencies and systemic toxicity. Their findings make the need for labeling all the more urgent, and the advice to buy certified organic all the more valid. Indeed, according to Dr. Seneff, 'glyphosate is possibly the most important factor in the development of multiple chronic diseases and conditions that have become prevalent in Westernized societies, including but not limited to:'

Autism	Gastrointestinal diseases such as inflammatory bowel disease, chronic diarrhea, colitis and Crohn's disease	Obesity
Allergies	Cardiovascular disease	Depression
Cancer	Infertility	Alzheimer's disease
Parkinson's disease	Multiple sclerosis	ALS, and more

How glyphosate worsens modern diseases: While Monsanto insists that Roundup is as safe to humans as aspirin, Seneff and Samsel's research tells a different story altogether. Their report, published in the journal Entropy, argues that glyphosate residues, found in most commonly consumed foods in the Western diet courtesy of GE sugar, corn, soy and wheat; '...enhance the damaging effects of other

*food-borne chemical residues and toxins in the environment
to disrupt normal body functions and induce disease.'*

*Interestingly, your gut bacteria are a key component of
glyphosate's mechanism of harm.*

*Monsanto has steadfastly claimed that Roundup is
harmless to animals and humans because the mechanism
of action it uses (which allows it to kill weeds), called the
shikimate pathway, is absent in all animals.*

*However, the shikimate pathway IS present in bacteria,
and that's the key to understanding how it causes such
widespread systemic harm in both humans and animals.*

*The bacteria in your body outnumber your cells by 10 to
1. For every cell in your body, you have 10 microbes of various
kinds, and all of them have the shikimate pathway, so they
will all respond to the presence of glyphosate!*

***Glyphosate causes extreme disruption of the
microbe's function and life cycle. What's worse, glyphosate
preferentially affects beneficial bacteria, allowing
pathogens to overgrow and take over. At that point, your
body also has to contend with the toxins produced by
the pathogens. Once the chronic inflammation sets in,
you're well on your way toward chronic and potentially
debilitating disease."(23)***

In the interview above, Dr. Seneff reviews a variety of
chronic diseases, explaining how glyphosate contributes to each
condition. To learn more, I urge you to listen to it in its entirety. It
is quite eye opening. She continues:

*"The overlooked component of toxicity: The research
reveals that glyphosate inhibits cytochrome P450 (CYP)
enzymes, a large and diverse group of enzymes that catalyze
the oxidation of organic substances. This, the authors state,
is 'an overlooked component of its toxicity to mammals.' One
of the functions of CYP enzymes is to detoxify xenobiotics,
chemical compounds found in a living organism that are not
normally produced or consumed by the organism in question.*

*By limiting the ability of these enzymes to detoxify
foreign chemical compounds, glyphosate enhances the
damaging effects of chemicals and environmental toxins you
may be exposed to."*

Dr. Stephanie Seneff has been conducting research at MIT
for over three decades. She also has an undergraduate degree in
biology from MIT and a minor in food and nutrition, and has been
interviewed about her groundbreaking insights into the critical
importance of sulfur in human health. Not surprisingly, this
latest research also touches on sulfur, and how it is affected by
glyphosate from food.

*"We show how interference with CYP enzymes acts
synergistically with disruption of the biosynthesis of aromatic
amino acids by gut bacteria, as well as impairment in serum
sulfate transport," the authors write.*

*Consequences are most of the diseases and
conditions associated with a Western diet, which include
gastrointestinal disorders, obesity, diabetes, heart disease,
depression, autism, infertility, cancer and Alzheimer's
disease. The recent alarming increase in all of these health*

issues can be traced back to a combination of gut dysbiosis, impaired sulfate transport, and suppression of the activity of the various members of the cytochrome P450 (CYP) family of enzymes."

The Roundup-autism connection: *Since the 1980s, Dr. Seneff has been passionate about teasing out potential causes of autism, after seeing what it was like for a close friend whose son was diagnosed. She points out the clear correlations between increased glyphosate use over recent years (the result of genetically engineered crops causing weed resistance, necessitating ever-larger amounts to be used) and skyrocketing autism rates.*

The rate of autism has risen so quickly, there can be no doubt that it has an environmental cause. Our genes simply cannot mutate fast enough to account for the rapid rise we are now seeing. The latest statistics released by the CDC on March 20 [2014] show that 1 in 50 children in the US now fall within the autism spectrum 2,3, with a 5:1 boy to girl ratio. Just last year [2013] the CDC reported a rate of 1 in 88, which represented a 23 percent increase since 2010, and 78 percent since 2007. Meanwhile, I remember when the incidence of autism in the US was only 1 in 10,000—just short of 30 years ago!

Dr. Seneff identified two key problems in autism that are unrelated to the brain yet clearly associated with the condition, both of which are linked with glyphosate exposure (starting at 10 minutes into the interview, she gives an in-depth explanation of how glyphosate causes the many symptoms associated with autism):

1) Gut dysbiosis (imbalances in gut bacteria, inflammation, leaky gut, food allergies such as gluten intolerance)

2)Disrupted sulfur metabolism / sulfur and sulfate deficiency.

Interestingly, certain microbes in your body actually break down glyphosate, which is a good thing. However, a byproduct of this action is ammonia, and children with autism tend to have significantly higher levels of ammonia in their blood than the general population. Ditto for those with Alzheimer's disease. In your brain, ammonia causes encephalitis, i.e. brain inflammation.

Another devastating agent you really do not want in your body is formaldehyde, which a recent nutritional analysis discovered is present in genetically engineered corn at a level that is 200 times the amount that studies have determined to be toxic to animals. Formaldehyde destroys DNA and can cause cancer.

Other research backing up the Roundup-autism link is that from former US Navy staff scientist Dr. Nancy Swanson. She has a Ph.D. in physics, holds five US patents and has authored more than 30 scientific papers and two books on women in science. Ten years ago, she became seriously ill, and in her journey to regain her health she turned to organic foods. Not surprisingly (for those in the know) her symptoms dramatically improved. This prompted her to start investigating genetically engineered foods.

She has meticulously collected statistics on glyphosate usage and various diseases and conditions, including autism. A more perfect match-up between the rise in glyphosate usage and incidence of autism is hard to imagine. To access her published articles and reports, please visit Sustainable Pulse, a European website dedicated to exposing the hazards of genetically engineered foods.

Vitamin D deficiency has suddenly appeared on the horizon, like oh my God, half the country has vitamin D deficiency. There's a real epidemic going on. And you have to wonder whether that's also coinciding with this increased exposure (to glyphosate). Because it's not just that more glyphosate is being used, it's that more of it is being soaked up, because we have all these GMOs that are happy to just soak it up and they don't die.

One of the ways that the protective effect of sunlight exposure makes sense is recognizing the critical role that vitamin D plays in sulfate homeostasis. A study in mice found that activated vitamin D prevented sulfate wasting from the kidney in urine, and mice engineered to have defective vitamin D receptors (or with vitamin D deficiency) had significantly reduced serum sulfate levels, which were associated with sulfate depletion in the skeleton. Children with autism have high sulfate in their urine but low serum sulfate levels, which clearly indicates both generic sulfate deficiency and vitamin D deficiency.

Glyphosate, the elephant in the room: Dr. Stephanie Seneff began paying attention to glyphosate after she had been intensely researching autism for five or six years. Glyphosate is a broad-spectrum systemic herbicide (known to the world under its trade name Roundup®). Among its many nefarious health effects, glyphosate disrupts the way the body manages sulfur.

In the process of examining all the known toxic chemicals in the environment and assessing which one(s) would be most likely to be causal for autism—given the specific co-morbidities associated with autism—Dr. Seneff found that glyphosate matched up almost perfectly.

Both glyphosate and autism are associated with low melatonin, impaired sulfur metabolism (and low serum sulfate), low vitamin D, sleep disorders, disrupted gut bacteria, and more. Glyphosate—already a very dangerous chemical on its own—causes aluminum to be much more toxic. Glyphosate and aluminum can be viewed as "partners in crime," working synergistically with one another. This partnership plays out in several ways:

First, glyphosate preferentially kills beneficial bacteria in the gut, which allows pathogens such as C. difficile to overgrow. Not only does this lead to leaky gut syndrome, but C. difficile produces something called p-Cresol, a phenolic compound that is toxic to other microbes via its ability to interfere with metabolism. (C. difficile is one of only a few bacteria able to ferment tyrosine into p-Cresol.) As it happens, *p-Cresol also promotes aluminum uptake by cells. P-Cresol is a known biomarker for autism and is an important factor in kidney failure, which leads to aluminum retention in tissues and eventually to dementia.*

Glyphosate also serves to increase aluminum toxicity by "caging" aluminum to promote its entry into the body. Glyphosate promotes calcium uptake by voltage-activated channels, which allow aluminum to gain entry as a calcium mimetic. Aluminum then promotes calcium loss from bones, contributing to pineal gland calcification.

Bringing melatonin back into the discussion, glyphosate interferes with what is known as the shikimate pathway. Although humans do not have the shikimate pathway, our gut flora do, and we depend on our gut flora to supply us with essential amino acids and many other things. Disruption of the shikimate pathway in our gut results in depletion of tryptophan, which is the sole precursor to melatonin. Besides needing melatonin to transport sulfate into the brain, we also need melatonin to reduce heavy metal toxicity. Where supplies of melatonin are adequate, melatonin will bind to aluminum, cadmium, copper, iron, and lead, and reduce their toxicity. Where melatonin is low, a lot of damage can result.

Roundup® is the number one herbicide in use in the US and, increasingly, around the world. Unfortunately, its use has increased further in lockstep with 'Roundup-Ready' genetically engineered crops, including genetically modified (GM) mainstay crops such as soy and corn.

Dr. Seneff believes that when children are overexposed to glyphosate, especially through consumption of the GM foods that are widely prevalent in the American diet, they are more likely to react badly to vaccination.

Summary: Taken together, the body of evidence elegantly assembled by Dr. Seneff supports her hypothesis that the epidemic levels of autism (and other diseases such as Alzheimer's disease) currently seen in the Western world are caused by a severe deficiency in sulfate supplies to the brain. Under optimal circumstances, the pineal gland can synthesize sulfate stimulated by sunlight and deliver it via melatonin sulfate to the brain. However, aluminum, mercury, and glyphosate are working synergistically to derail this process, and sunlight deficiency (exacerbated by the misguided use of sunscreens containing aluminum nanoparticles) is further contributing to the pathology.

How to protect yourself and your family from this systemic poison: It's important to understand that the glyphosate sprayed on conventional and genetically engineered crops actually becomes systemic throughout the plant, so it cannot be washed off. It's inside the plant. For example, genetically engineered corn has been found to contain 13 parts per million of glyphosate, compared to zero in non-GMO corn. At 13 ppm, GMO corn contains more than 18 times the 'safe' level of glyphosate set by the EPA. Organ damage in animals has occurred at levels as low as 0.1 ppm. If that's not reason enough to become a label reader to avoid anything with corn in it, such as corn oil or high fructose corn syrup, I don't know what is.

You would also be wise to stop using Roundup around your home, where children and pets can come into contact with it simply by walking across the area.

Until the US requires genetically engineered foods to be labeled, the only way you can avoid GE ingredients is to make whole, fresh organic foods the bulk of your diet, and to only buy 100 percent USDA certified organic processed foods. Meats need to be grass-fed or pastured to make sure the animals were not fed GE corn or soy feed. Last but not least, do not confuse the "natural" label with organic standards.

The natural label is not based on any standards and is frequently misused by sellers of GE products. Growers and manufacturers of organic products bearing the USDA seal, on the other hand, have to meet the strictest standards of any of the currently available organic labels. In order to qualify as organic, a product must be grown and processed using organic farming methods that recycle resources and promote biodiversity. Crops must be grown without synthetic pesticides, bioengineered genes, petroleum-based fertilizers, or sewage sludge-based fertilizers." (23a.)

For the full interview go to: http://articles.mercola.com/sites/articles/archive/2013/06/09/monsanto-roundup-herbicide.aspx

Monsanto Feeding The World

Now let us look at Monsanto's pretentious claims to "feed the world" in this excerpt from an Interview with Claire Robinson by Jeffrey Smith of www.gmwatch.org.

"In order to feed the world, GM crops would really have to do at least two things. They'd have to yield more than the non-GM equivalent crop and they'd have to cope with stresses, like extreme weather conditions and bad soils and so forth, better than non-GM crops. The evidence is that GM crops don't do either of these things. The yield for GM crops is no better than for the equivalent non-GM crops. There have been increases in yield for the major crops over the past few decades, but these are entirely due to conventional breeding improvements.

In fact, we shouldn't be surprised that GM crops don't have higher yields on the whole, because they were never engineered for higher yields. The two GM crops on the market now that dominate the biotechnology market are crops to resist the applications of herbicides so they can absorb herbicides and not die. Also, there are the GM crops that produce their own herbicide. This is claimed to reduce the chemical insecticide use, which of course it does, but people forget that these plants are in fact biological pesticides. So when you or our livestock are eating these crops, they're actually eating a pesticide.

The other claim for GM crops in this 'feeding the world' myth is that they're somehow going to cope with extreme weather conditions like droughts or floods. The truth of the matter is that flood tolerance and drought tolerance are actually complex traits. They are not the kind of simple traits that can be engineered into a crop by moving around one or two genes. They are what are known as complex traits. They are the product of interactions between genes that we really

don't understand, and conventional breeding has been very,
very successful in producing crops that are very resilient to
these extreme weather conditions". (24)

Corporations told the farmer's decades ago that they'd
be better off practicing what's known today as agro business
practices, using their (Monsanto, Dow etc.) pesticide to eradicate
bugs and weeds instead of planting companion plants known
to be healthier and more effective to the plants and leaving
hedgerows* on the exterior of the crops.

We cannot ignore the consequences of how our actions
affect the world around us when we sit down to the dinner table
to nourish ourselves.

"To get to know a country, you must have direct contact
with the earth. It's futile to gaze at the world through a car
window." - Albert Einstein

Many of today's CEOs and leaders are indeed gazing at our
world through car windows. Here is another scenario to consider,
or food for thought:

- GMO seeds with insecticides embedded in the DNA are
  used to grow our foods.
- Corn, soy, and grains grown from those seeds are fed to
  the farm animals used for human protein sources.
- Due to soil erosion, depletion of minerals and trace
  minerals the soil is no longer viable or sustainable.
- Fruits, vegetables, grains and animals fed by these
  sources are deficient in minerals, trace minerals and the
  nutrition our creator intended them to have.

- We blindly consume those fruits, vegetables, grains and proteins, believing that we are being nourished, because we are told our government would not do anything to hurt us. And "we" believe it?
- Our bodies don't recognize what we eat as real food because the food no longer has the same DNA structure and sequences originally intended to nourish our cells. AND it's full of insecticides.
- We, and I mean all humans, animals and insects on the planet, although mostly in the USA, are getting sicker every day, creating a great market for the medical, pharmaceutical and supplement industries.
- The pharmaceutical industry funds the medical schools, (25) where our future doctors learn little, if anything about preventative health care, including the benefits of eating organic, non GMO foods. If the schools did teach this to their medical students, and the medical profession taught this to their patients, the pharmaceutical industry would largely go out of business.
- We continue to get sicker, supporting Western medicine in a reactionary, rather than preventative mindset against disease.
- Big agro-businesses like Monsanto and Dow chemical continue to spew out billions of gallons of toxins for the general consumption of the planet.
- These companies and the pharmaceuticals pour millions of dollars into the government to keep us in the dark via support of our elected politicians and grossly financed

misinformation campaigns. (read 'Altered Genes, Twisted Truths' by Steven M. Drucker)

The FDA, whose purported intent is to keep unsafe foods and chemicals out of our food chain, is in bed with those same agro-business companies, thus giving us a false sense of security with half-truths and lies about the safety and efficacy of our food sources, GMOs in particular.

When is it time to say, "I'm mad as hell and I'm not going to take this anymore!" (26) These companies are making Billions (that's with a capitol B), literally poisoning people and the planet.

In my interview with Dana Murdock, she further stated:

"In 1968 I was in Idaho Falls, Idaho when corporate farms started buying up all the potato farms up there. Frank Church was still the Senator and fighting for the farmers. Simplot, the big fertilizer company originating in Idaho, was in support of the corporate farms. All of the farmers in the Idaho Falls area hauled all their potatoes to the middle of a big field and burned them! This was a gigantic fire, bigger than anything I've ever seen in my life! Rather than sell potatoes for less than it cost to produce them, because the corporate farms were selling them at below production costs to put small farmers out of business, the farmers just burned them."

Russet Burbank Potatoes, which are the only potatoes McDonalds will buy, were sprayed with a toxic pesticide in order to avoid net necrosis, a little brown line or spot inside the potato. The only way to eliminate net necrosis is to eliminate an aphid, which means you have to use the pesticide known as Monitor. This pesticide is so toxic that farmers using it on their potato fields would not go into their own fields for five days after they sprayed. After harvesting, these potatoes had to be quarantined for six weeks in order to off gas the pesticide. Until this off gassing occurred, no human, animal or plant was to come into contact with the potatoes because of extreme toxicity. Obviously, these potatoes were not edible during the off-gassing period". (27)

Monitor Pesticide

Hazards to humans and domestic animals (listed on the actual bag) for Monitor are:

"Do not inhale. Do not get on skin. Do not take internally. Fatal if swallowed. Fatal if inhaled. May be fatal if absorbed through the skin. Causes irreversible eye damage. Do not breathe vapor or spray mist. Do not get in eyes, on skin or on clothing.

Environmental hazards: This product is extremely toxic to birds, mammals, and aquatic invertebrates. Do not apply directly to water, or to areas where surface water is present or to inter-tidal areas below the mean watermark. Drift and runoff may be hazardous to aquatic organisms in neighboring areas". (28)

Is it realistic to presume that none of this pesticide has trickled into the water system or killed valuable birds, bees, or butterflies visiting the fields? Should we assume that those residues are gone from the very potatoes you're consuming with your Big Mac? Probably not.

So here we are, caught in the middle of a spiraling funnel of greed and short-sightedness that continues to flush our health down the proverbial toilet, while lining the pockets of the corporations and politicians.

You may be asking yourself how our country can get off this mutant-hamster wheel? There is no easy, short-term fix for these problems, because our soil is so depleted that it will take years to nurture it back to its former glorious bounty. The good news is that it can be done, and thousands of farmers worldwide are beginning to fight back against the mainstream chemical mindset, planting non GMO seeds inherited from the original seeds used for millennia.

According to agricultural economist John Ikerd in an email communication with Steven M. Druker, "Although these changes couldn't be made immediately, they could still be achieved rather quickly". – Altered Genes, Twisted Truth, pages 401,2.

In 1900, there were approximately 30,000 farmers, in 1960 that number was down to 16,000, about 8.5 percent of the American workforce and in 1990 that number was down to less than 2 percent of the population. There are a growing number of people returning to small-scale farming in an effort to get back to growing real foods.

For an excellent example of long-term successful farming practices, read the article "Indigenous Knowledge Re-valued in Andean Agriculture"(29)

As stewards of the earth, our responsibility is to care for and nourish the soil. We used to have a more symbiotic relationship to the soil that has been all but lost by our separation from the very foods we consume. From the soil to the stomach, we have no clue where our food is grown or how it's processed before we put it in our cart and run it through our sacred, god given vessels. So what exactly IS the matter in food today?

Chapter 3

WTF Is the Matter In Food?

'The Greek word 'diaita' refers to a routine or way of life. This too, is a word that the term 'diet' comes from. The 'dia' beginning in this word and the Latin word alike refers to the need to take something apart as well. This is to create a better lifestyle that entails removing unhealthy foods and attitudes from one's life." (30)

When you consume foods that lead to health your *diet* is a good one. When you consume foods that are full of chemicals and pesticides, and don't come from *light* (photosynthesis or sunlight), you're eating Dark foods with no nutritional value.

Man-Made Ingredients/Additives

'The more I learn about food additives and their effects on human health, the harder it is for me to wrap my brain around how this kind of science even exists. What we do to our foods these days is food chemistry gone bad." (31)

Here's the list of ingredients taken off the back of a popular ice cream label. You *might* be feeding this to your loved ones:

- Propylene glycol
- Ethyl acetate
- Yellow dye #5
- Hydrogenated oils
- High fructose corn syrup
- Dry milk solids
- Caroxymethyl cellulose
- Butyraldehyde and amyl acetate are additives in some commercial ice creams.
- Diethyl glycol, a chemical used to take the place of eggs, which is also used in anti-freeze and paint removers.
- Aldehyde C-17, flavoring for cherry ice cream, is an inflammable liquid used in dyes, plastics, and rubber.
- Piperonal, commonly used in place of vanilla, is a lice killer.
- Ethyl Acetate, a pineapple flavor, is also used to clean leather and textiles.
- Ethyl Acetate's vapor has been known to cause chronic lung, liver, and heart damage.
- Mono and diglicerides
- Disodium phosphate
- Benzyl acetate
- Mono stearate
- Propylene glycol
- Sodium benzoate
- Polysorbate 80
- Potassium sorbate
- Modified cornstarch
- Soy lecithin

GRAS (Generally Regarded As Safe)

Most of these additives are on the GRAS (generally recognized as safe) list by the FDA, but this most certainly doesn't mean they aren't harmful. Your question should be: Are any of these ingredients even necessary to what should be a wholesome treat? Since the FDA does not require ice cream makers to label all of their ingredients, you may even find other, more deadly ones.

If you were using real cream, egg yolks, and pure maple or organic vanilla syrup, your ice cream could be a delicious way to get healthy fat, calcium, enzymes, vitamins, and minerals. Make your own ice cream. It's relatively simple with an electric ice cream maker or a blender. My grandkids and I make frozen treats in the summer months out of fresh fruits, liquid stevia for sweetener, coconut milk and real organic, non-GMO cream.

Canola Oil

According to Dee McCaffrey in her book 'The Science of Skinny':

> "There's no such thing as a canola. The real name of
> canola oil is rapeseed oil. The natural, untainted rapeseed
> is high in heart-healthy mono-unsaturated fats and also
> contains omega-3 fats. The problem is that about two-thirds
> of the mono-unsaturated fat in natural, untainted rapeseed
> is a type called erucic acid, which has been associated with
> heart lesions and other ailments. To remove the erucic acid,
> Canadian plant breeders had to genetically engineer
> The new oil, called lear oil, was slow to catch on in
> the United States. To be marketable, it had to be renamed.
> Neither Lear oil or rape oil were very enticing terms, so
> the industry settled on canola, for the quote Canadian oil,'

because most of the engineered rapeseed at that time was grown in Canada.

Via genetic engineering, the industry had managed to manipulate rapeseed to make a perfect oil -- very low in saturated fat and rich in monounsaturated fat. As a bonus, canola oil contains about 10 percent omega-3 fatty acids, which had been shown to be beneficial for the heart and immune system. Since most Americans are deficient in omega-3 fats, the oil was a dream come true for health-conscious consumers. But how healthy is it really?

Although rapeseed has been used as a source of oil since ancient times in China and India, the way it was historically obtained, using small stone presses to press out the oil at low temperatures, rendered a fresh, healthy oil that was consumed immediately. It has even been proven by recent studies that the erucic acid in rapeseed oil does not create heart lesions, as long as a significant amount of saturated fat is also part of the diet. In fact, erucic acid is helpful in the treatment of the wasting disease adrenoleukodystrophy and was the magic ingredient in Lorenzo's oil (a combination of olive oil and rapeseed oils).

However, the way we now process canola oil, and most other oils for that matter, is a different thing entirely, rendering them very unhealthy. Because canola oil, and all modern vegetable and seed oils (e.g., soybean oil and corn oil), are so unstable, it is nearly impossible to keep them from turning rancid. So they have to be highly processed and refined at high heat (400 to 500 degrees Fahrenheit) and treated with chemical solvents such as hexane, a fluid *also used in dry cleaning. Traces of hexane remain in the oil, even after considerable refining. The refinement process involves bleaching and degumming, which require the use of additional chemicals of questionable safety. Canola oil contains a good amount of omega-3 fats, which easily become rancid and foul smelling when subjected to oxygen and high heat, so the oil also has to be deodorized. The deodorization process converts a large portion of the healthy omega-3 three fats into very unhealthy trans fats. Trans fats are formed at 320 degrees Fahrenheit, so imagine how much damage is done at 400 to 500 degrees. Although the Canadian government lists the trans-fat content of canola oil at a minimal 0.2 percent, research at the University of Florida at Gainesville found trans-fat levels as high as 4.6 percent in commercial liquid canola oil. The consumer has no clue about the presence of trans fats in canola oil because they are not listed on the label."*

- Dee McAffrey, CDC (31)

<u>Dee McCaffrey Interview</u>

When discussing the GMO right to know, and food issues in the world, this is what Dee had to say;

"My feeling is that it can't be talked about enough, because information still hasn't reached the mainstream, and we still haven't gotten enough people to vote for labeling laws. That tells me that not enough people are educated about it, or they don't understand it. They don't have the information to make educated choices because all they are getting is the campaign slander from the Monsanto side. If this is all people

*are hearing they are not really hearing the real message of
what this is all about.*

*I teach an introductory holistic nutrition class at
the Southwest Institute of Healing Arts in Tempe, AZ. It's
an intro class, so some students come in with knowledge
of GMOs, but the majority of them have heard the term
and don't know what it means. They leave the class very
enlightened with a sense of 'Oh my gosh, what do we do?' "*

With regard to choosing two subjects that relate to food
consumption in our country and the relative dis-ease, Dee states:

*"Obesity is certainly one of the primary diseases that are
directly related to our food. In addition, the other one is heart
disease. Heart disease is the number one killer, and obesity
is probably right behind it in terms of all the complications
that come from being obese. I see a correlation between
obesity leading to heart disease mainly because one of the
main contributing factors to obesity is consumption of refined
sugars. Sugar also leads to heart disease in a number of ways,
because it leads to higher triglycerides and fats in the blood.
That is what leads to heart disease. However, statistically
scientists have now proven that sugar consumption, even if
it doesn't make a person obese, can still lead to heart disease.
We're seeing the adverse effects of sugar consumption even
in people who are considered normal weight. It doesn't
necessarily go hand-in-hand, but it's still a killer.*

*The people that I work with as a nutrition counselor
are mostly obese or over weight. This is the area that I see
most people struggling. I see heart disease in my family, my*

father having had a quintuple bi-pass, and his mother died of a stroke at fifty-two. I get concerned because my siblings are over-weight and both smoke. That is why it's of particular concern to me. I try to educate them, without being preachy.

With regard to GMOs in particular, I feel that GMOs are probably one of the most significant health threats that we are facing now in our country, and in our world. GMOs to me are just like any other man-made thing that we're eating. For instance, in processed foods we are eating trans-fats, and artificial flavors. It's much worse with GMOs, because we're toying with the genetic material of food that was already perfect. Because our bodies don't recognize the DNA sequencing when we eat those foods, our bodies reject them. This rejection is showing up in many different ways. The thing that I find the most abhorrent about it is that they have NOT been tested to see what the long-term, or even short-term effects would be. They're trying to cover up all of the science that has already been done on it, and any scientists who want to talk about it get hushed up or discredited. I feel like it's a big secret, a big problem, and there isn't enough exposure about it. If people really knew what GMOs were, how they affect us, and about some of the scientific studies that have been done, they would be more concerned about it.

When you see all of the links to the different health issues, like leaky gut syndrome, allergies, autism, and heart disease, there are so many things that can be linked back to GMOs, mainly because the body doesn't recognize them. The body has never seen that sequence of DNA, so it just doesn't know what to do with it. Our bodies respond to GMOs as *if they're foreign, because they are! Because the body does not recognize GMOs, it gets inflammation in several areas. That is what is creating all the autoimmune diseases. It's out of control now because it's so hard to know where all these things are coming from.*

When I'm trying to help someone with their nutrition, they have all these issues, and it's so difficult to know where to start. The first place I tell them to start is to buy non-GMO groceries, and see what happens from there. Usually many things clear up for people when they go non-GMO. For many people it's very difficult because GMOs are so pervasive. They're in so many things, because we don't have adequate, or any labeling, that people don't know where to start. How many people are going to take the time to read every label for everything they buy? What it all comes back to is, don't buy things that are packaged. Shop the perimeter of your store. If you are just buying whole foods, there is less GMO exposure.

About ten years ago my brother had sever diverticulitis, and had a portion of his large intestine surgically removed because it was so inflamed. After that he decided to become a vegetarian and clean up his diet. He did really well for a while but then drifted back to old eating habits. Now he has type-two diabetes because his blood sugar levels skyrocketed and he is obese. I see how he is trying to eat better and take care of himself, but I think it is hard because it has become such a habit to eat certain foods. There is an addictive quality to most foods in the grocery store. I see that with many people, the addiction to the food is really the most difficult part of staying healthy. I feel those food addictions will take his life too soon. Ideally, he should live a long life, but because he is only in his forties, and already has all these serious issues, that is probably not realistic.

I feel that people need to be educated about the amount of sugar in the food they are eating, as well as the chemical nature of the food. Most people do not read the ingredients, and therefore have no clue that they are just eating a bunch of chemicals. Look at the ingredients list on the 'Lunchables' for kids. They have thirty-five different ingredients in a crackers and cheese package. People think, oh it's just crackers and cheese, but it's not. It is not even real! I think people would have more awareness if they were educated about the chemicals in foods, and how they affect us. They should also be aware that some of the chemicals we allow in our foods are not allowed in other countries. Other countries have taken measures to get the chemicals out of their foods because they know that they are harmful.

In our country, the FDA says that those foods are not harmful because there is not enough evidence to prove it. That is simply not true!

We need awareness on national news and more mainstream television. Sometimes Dr. Oz has good information on his program, but it is not enough.

I have a friend that told me when she first heard me talking about all of this; she would go to other people and tout what she had learned. She would tell them 'trusted the Government to keep me safe, and now I understand that lack of good health wasn't my fault. I thought I was doing the right thing, eating fat-free, low fat, sugar free and all the *things they tell us to do. And yet all those foods are filled with chemicals that are really harmful, make you fat and cause high blood sugar.' She was one of those intelligent people who trusted and assumed that anything that is in our food supply was safe. Otherwise, it wouldn't be allowed, right? That is what we should be able to think.*

I do feel that there is a lot more awareness today than there was just a few years ago. Grass roots movements, bloggers, movies and books are telling the public about what is in their foods. Nevertheless, we need more. I used to feel like a lone voice twenty years ago spouting off all this information, but now I am one of many to give voice. If somebody didn't believe me ten or twenty years ago, maybe they will now, since there's more credibility in more voices."

EAFUS - Everything Added To Food

Listed in the EAFUS (Everything Added to Food in the United States) document of the FDA's database are more than 3,900 ingredients of *mostly* synthetic things added to our foods. Here's just a few listed under the A's:

"ACRYLAMIDE-ACRYLIC ACID RESIN: Acrylic resins are a group of related thermoplastic or thermosetting plastic substances derived from acrylic acid, methacrylic acid or other related compounds. Polymethol acrylate is an acrylic resin used in an emulsed form for laquer, textile finishes, adhesives and, when mixed with clay, to gloss paper."

WTF? Why is this in our food?

"ACETALDEHYDE, BUTYL PHENETHYL ACETAL Functional use(s) - flavor and fragrance agents. Has a green type odor and a green type flavor" [I am not clear on how an additive can have green type odor or flavor]. *The Oral/Parenteral Toxicity is Not Determined, the Dermal Toxicity is not determined and the Inhalation Toxicity is not determined."*

Under the letter M:

"MALTODEXTRIN is a polysaccharide that is used as a food. It is produced from starch by partial hydrolysis and is usually found as a white hygroscopic spray-dried powder. Maltodextrin is easily digestible, being absorbed as rapidly as glucose, and might be either moderately sweet or almost flavorless. It is commonly used for the production of sodas and candy. It can also be found as an ingredient in a variety of other processed foods."

"Maltodextrin can be enzymatically derived from any starch. In the US, this starch is usually corn; in Europe, it is commonly wheat. Some individuals suffering from gluten intolerance may be concerned by the presence of wheat-derived maltodextrin but it is highly unlikely to contain significant (20mg/kg or 20ppm) amounts of gluten. If wheat is used to make maltodextrin, it does not need to appear on the label. Maltodextrin derived from cereals containing

gluten is exempt from labeling, as set out in AnnexIIIa of EC Directive 2000/13." (Wikepedia)

When I read the canister of my favorite protein drink to find that it indeed has Maltodextrin listed in the ingredients, I reluctantly decided to stop drinking it after 12 years. Then I read ingredients listed in the same company's women's supplements I have used for 12 years and found they have carnauba wax in them.

*It is known as 'queen of waxes' and in its pure state, usually comes in the form of hard yellow-brown flakes. It is obtained from the leaves of the carnauba palm by collecting and drying them, beating them to loosen the wax, then refining and **bleaching the wax**." (Wikipedia)*

I will *not* knowingly ingest bleach or other synthetic substances. This is the real problem. How do we really know what it is in everything we eat unless we grow it ourselves?

I was recently looking for a good nutritional supplement in my local health food store and found several that purported to be "organic". On further reading of the "other ingredients" listed on the labels, I again found maltodextrin. So when did an ingredient obviously made or refined by humans/machines become organic?

Here is the ingredient list off the hot chocolate mix we used to give to our grandchildren after playing long hours in the snow: Refined sugar, corn syrup, modified whey, cocoa (processed with alkali), hydrogenated coconut oil, nonfat milk, calcium carbonate, salt, dipotassium phosphate, mono and diglycerides, artificial flavor, carrageenan and lastly, whole milk. Now let us look at what these ingredients really are:

Refined Sugar: *is 99.8 percent pure sucrose balanced by nothing. This is where the term 'empty calories' comes from, calories with no nutrients (31)*

Corn Syrup: *has been called the "crack" of sweeteners and "liquid satin." It is highly addictive and contributes to the development of diabetes, liver disease, heart disease and obesity among other maladies. It is a highly processed syrup that is a far cry from the natural corn it's derived from." (32)*

Modified Whey: *is the liquid bi-product of cheese production. Every 10 units of full-fat milk will yield about one unit of cheese and nine units of fluid whey. Whey protein concentrate (WPC) is obtained by removing sufficient non-protein constituents from whey. Whey powder, WPC, and other modified whey products are all used in food products. (35)*

Cocoa (processed with alkali): is made by the *fermentation of fresh cacao beans, which decreases antioxidant content, as does the roasting of cacao beans and the treatment of cocoa powder with alkali. Processing with alkali is called dutching and it breaks down the flavanol antioxidants naturally found in cocoa and chocolate. The extent to which the flavanols are lost is related to how heavily the cocoa or chocolate is dutched. Dutched cocoa can be identified on the ingredient panel of a food when labeled as "cocoa processed with alkali." Unfortunately, food labels do not state the extent of alkalization of a cocoa powder, so you should choose a natural, non-alkalized cocoa for maximum antioxidants. (35)*

Hydrogenated Coconut Oil: *can lead to the same risk for stroke as it does for heart disease. "Just as the blood vessels are affected in the heart, they can also be affected in the brain. If blood vessels are blocked in the brain because of consuming a diet high in hydrogenated or saturated fats like hydrogenated coconut oil, this can lead to a stroke." (35) (This should however not be confused with the healthy benefits of extra virgin coconut oil).*

Calcium carbonate: *is the least usable form of calcium found in nature. Carbonate is such a bad chelator it cannot be considered as such. (WIKI Answers.com)*

Dipotassium Phosphate: *is a stable chemical compound used in various manufactured products (mostly food). It comes as an odorless, white crystal powder with a shelf life of about 12 months. It is deliquescent when exposed to moist air. Dipotassium phosphate, in combination with another EPA-approved compound (dipotassium phosphonate), is intended to control fungal plant diseases on turf, ornamentals, and non-bearing fruit and nut tree crops (that is, on trees that have not yet developed the edible crop). The active ingredient appears to have a mixed mode of action involving direct toxicity to the pathogen, aided by a boosting of the plant's defense mechanisms due the fertilizing properties of the compound. (35)*

Mono and diglycerides: *are composed of fatty acids, and may contain trans-fats, when those fatty acids are subjected to high-heat processing. The industry only* has to report trans-fat content from triglycerides--not from monoglycerides or diglycerides. However, trans-fats are formed when mono and diglycerides are manufactured. Manufactured, not grown or harvested, but constructed in a lab, just like partially hydrogenated oils. (35)

Artificial flavor: "The Food and Drug Administration does not require the companies that carefully manufacture flavor additives to disclose the ingredients that are in their product, as long as the chemicals used are 'generally regarded as safe' (GRAS). There are often more ingredients in the artificial flavoring than in the processed food that it is made for." (36)

Carrageenan: Research by Medical Researcher Dr. Joanne Tobacman has shown that exposure to carrageenan causes inflammation and that when we consume processed foods containing it, we ingest enough to cause inflammation in our bodies. She explained that all forms of carrageenan are capable of causing inflammation. This is bad news. We know that chronic inflammation is a root cause of many serious diseases including heart disease, Alzheimer's and Parkinson's diseases, and cancer. (37)

Don't you just want to run out and get some of this processed, powdered hot cocoa mix and add some refined sugar marshmallows to it for your loved ones?

These are the ingredients listed on a very popular children's cereal box that has the name fruit in it, but **no trace of actual fruit:** sugar, whole grain corn flour, wheat flour, whole grain oat flour, soluble corn fiber, contains 2 percent or less of partially hydrogenated vegetable oil (coconut, soybean and/or cottonseed),salt, red 40, natural flavor, blue 2, turmeric color, yellow 6, annatto color, blue 1, and BHT for freshness. This is what those ingredients really are:

> **Refined white sugar** *has no resemblance to its*
> *original form of sugar cane but in fact has been so "refined"*
> *and processed that it is poisonous to our bodies. (31)*

The dictionary defines "refined" as sophisticated, advanced, polished, improved, perfected, toned and enhanced. In fact, the process of refining sugar cane takes it from its beautiful, nutritious state and turns it into a substance that is now found to be more addictive than heroin, depletes our calcium, suppresses our immune system, and leads to obesity, diabetes, and cancer. I find nothing sophisticated, improved or enhanced about that.

> **Whole grain flour,** *according to [CDC Dee*
> *McCaffrey], is "considered potentially troublesome because*
> *research has shown that it creates a brain chemical response*
> *in the form of increased serotonin levels. This is the same*
> *phenomenon that is seen in sugar addiction." (34)*

Are you beginning to see a dangerous pattern here? (See Chapter 7 for more information on the Gut Brain connection.)

Farmed Fish

As we learned from Doctors Smith, Seneff and Samsel in Chapter 2, there is also glyphosate in almost everything we now consume. Even the farm-raised fish that is now in your grocery stores are fed GM soy and corn. Have you ever seen any soy or corn growing in the ocean? If you starve fish or animals long enough, like us they will eat pretty much anything. Like cows, pigs and chickens they're grown in such tight quarters that they often get sick so they're fed antibiotics and pesticides to keep them alive long enough to get to reach a marketable size. These include tilapia, catfish, and "wild (note the word caught is omitted) Atlantic" salmon (not really wild but farmed in Canada, Alaska, and Norway), rainbow trout, cobia, tuna, eel and shrimp so far. So when you want to eat good seafood with beneficial Omegas and no glyphosate or other surprises, please buy "wild caught" fish and seafood only. My personal preferences are cod, smelt, sand dabs, halibut and wild caught salmon.

<u>Feeding the Hungry</u>

There are several well-meaning organizations out there trying to help starving or malnourished children all over the world. For example "No Kid Hungry" is funded by several of the better known food corporations that primarily sell processed, GMO foods. On their list of "partners" is Karo, Kelloggs, Nestle, Tyson and C & H sugar. Of the more than 50 partners listed on their web site, only one touted "fresh food". How are we helping our starving children if what we are feeding them is not actually nutritional whole food? As the authors and specialists you have already read so far have clearly stated, these products are hurting, not helping our bodies. Feeding processed GMO food to starving people is like putting a Band-Aid on a severed artery! This is NOT a move forward to feed hungry children, but will most likely cause irreparable, long-term disease as they move through their lives. Those diseases will then

GOD MADE ORGANICS, NOT GMOS

need professional, medical help. You see where I'm going with this?

This reminds me of a time in the Reagan administration when the government was giving away surplus cheese to the poor and elderly. I believe my mother referred to it as a "senior euthanasia program."

December 22, 1981, Ronald Reagan wrote:

"I am authorizing today the immediate release of 30 million pounds from the CCC inventory. The cheese will be delivered to the States that request it and will be distributed free to the needy by nonprofit organizations.

The 1981 farm bill I signed today will slow the rise in price support levels, but even under this bill, surpluses will continue to pile up. A total of more than 560 million pounds of cheese has already been consigned to warehouses, so more distributions may be necessary as we continue our drive to root out waste in government and make the best possible use of our nation's resources." (38)

These programs bring to mind another favorite saying of Mother's when she was the director of the (then new) Senior Citizens Center in Palm Springs CA.: "There is an epidemic of anal, cranial inversion (head up the ass)."

Chapter 4

· ·

How About Those Prescription Drug Side Effects?

Now let us take a closer look at just a few of the prescription drugs available today, because if you and your loved ones are consuming the processed and GM products listed in chapter 3, eventually you'll be prescribed some of the lovely drugs below.

The FDA Define Drugs

The FDA's legal definition of a drug is "anything that diagnoses, cures, mitigates, treats, or prevents a disease."

"The problem with this definition is that there are numerous substances, as readily available and benign as found on our spice racks, which have been proven by countless millennia of human experience to mitigate, prevent and in some cases cure disease, and which cannot be called drugs according to the FDA.

How can this be? Well, the FDA has assumed for itself Godlike power, requiring that its official approval be obtained before any substance can legally be used in the prevention and treatment of disease." (39)

Drug Prescription Commercials

"... commercials for the arthritis medication Celebrex feature a narrator trying to persuade viewers that even with all of the complications (including heart failure) that can arise from using the drug, they should still ask for a prescription for it. What really takes the cake; however, are the visuals which consist entirely of roto scoped scenes with the lines being made of fine print of the drug's consequences!" (40)

Prescription Drug TV Ads by Vaughn Aubuchon:

"Here is a summary list of DTC (Direct-To-Consumer) prescription drug TV ads, along with their published adverse side effects. Your doctor does NOT know everything. Your doctor simply repeats what the pharmaceutical companies' literature says. MOST doctors ARE PAID to push pharmaceutical drugs. Kiddie Prozac Doctors Took Millions From Drug Makers. Drug manufacturers seek to minimize and trivialize the adverse side effects of the drugs they produce. To present a balanced picture, this page highlights these adverse side effects. In each case below, the official information is quoted verbatim, (fair use) from the drug companies' websites. Conclusion - What's the point?

How many of the latest TV ads will eventually be pulled due to adverse side effects? About 1 out of 3. You will find out when the ongoing, d-facto, long-term drug safety tests are completed **ON YOU!** *You will be protected, just as soon as enough other hapless individuals have suffered devastating ill effects. It does not pay to be an early 'adopter' in this business.*

The FDA works the same way as the FAA--only tragedy
evokes action". (41)

Drug Side Effects

The following is a short list of prescription drugs and their
possible side effects from Vaughn Aubuchon's website:

"Cialis: *Prescribed for erectile dysfunction. Brief side*
effects: Permanent, partial blindness. OFFICIAL: Unsafe
drop in blood pressure. Don't drink alcohol. Dizziness,
headache and upset stomach, backache or muscle ache,
erection lasting more than 4 hours (priapism), prostate
problems or high blood pressure.

*____*****Crestor**: *Statin and off-label uses. Brief side effects:*
Unexplained muscle pain, weakness, liver problems,
constipation, abdominal pain, nausea, food interactions, drug
interactions.

*____**OFFICIAL: Important safety information about*
Crestor: Unexplained muscle pain or weakness. Other
medications, liver problems, muscle aches, constipation,
weakness, abdominal pain and nausea.

*____*****Ditropan**: *Bladder control and off label uses.*

*____**OFFICIAL: Important safety information:*
Hypersensitivity to the drug substance or other components
of the product. The incidence of side effects reported more
commonly by patients treated with DITROPAN XL in
clinical trials using 10 mg daily compared to those permitting
doses of 5 to 30 mg daily was: dry mouth (29% vs 61%);
constipation (7% vs 13%); drowsiness (2% vs 12%); headache
(6% vs 10%); nausea (2% vs 9%); diarrhea (7% vs 9%); blurred

vision (1% vs 8%) and dizziness (4% vs 6%). Heat prostration (fever and heat stroke due to decreased sweating) can occur when anticholinergics such as oxybutynin are administered in hot weather.

Fosamax: *Osterporosis. Brief side effects: Heartburn, difficulty swallowing*

OFFICIAL: Selected cautionary information about FOSAMAX and FOSAMAX PLUS D

Disorders of the esophagus (the tube connecting the mouth with the stomach), not able to stand or sit upright for 30 minutes, serious kidney disease, low blood calcium or are allergic to FOSAMAX OR FOSAMAX PLUS D. Before use, talk to your doctor if you have, or have had stomach or digestive problems or problems with swallowing. New or worsening heartburn, difficult or painful swallowing or chest pain because these may be signs of serious upper digestive problems, which can include irritation, inflammation, or ulceration of the esophagus. Severe bone, joint, and/or muscle pain, stomach pain, indigestion/heartburn, or nausea."

Premarin: *Menopause. [This drug is a derivative of pregnant mare's urine, authors note] Brief side effects: Vaginitis, leg cramps, painful menstruation.*

OFFICIAL: Vaginitis due to yeast or other causes, vaginal bleeding, painful menstruation and leg cramps. Breast pain/enlargement, leg cramps, vaginal spotting, vaginal discomfort, breast pain, vaginitis, and itching. [I don't know what's worse, these side effects or the hot flashes. Both cause lack of sleep and irritability! Author's note]

Procrit: *Anemia. Brief side effects: Hypertension, increased death rate, seizures, thrombosis! [People still take this! Author's note].*

OFFICIAL:(Presented as a graphic only on the Procrit website, so search engines cannot read it.)

The following is from the National institute of Health; 'What side effects can this medication cause?'

Epoetin **(Procrit)** *may cause side effects. Tell your doctor if any of these symptoms are severe or do not go away: Headache, joint or muscle pain, upset stomach, vomiting, indigestion or 'heartburn,'stomach pain, diarrhea, constipation, runny nose, sneezing, difficulty falling asleep or staying asleep.'*

'Some side effects can be serious' [like the first ones aren't? Author's note]. The following symptoms are uncommon, but if you experience any of them, call your doctor immediately: Leg pain or swelling, shortness of breath, coughing up blood, cough that won't go away, blue-grey color or darkening around the mouth or nails, dizziness, fainting, blurred vision, temporary confusion, slow or difficult speech, loss of memory or ability to concentrate, hallucinating (seeing things or hearing voices that do not exist), extreme tiredness, seizures, weakness, numbness, heaviness, or tingling in arms or legs, floppiness or loss of muscle tone, lack of energy, increased or rapid heart rate [those nonexistent voices would do that for most people, Author's note], irregular heartbeat, chest pain or tightness, excessive sweating, fever, sore throat,

chills, cough, and other signs of infection, rash, hives, itching,
swelling of the face, throat, tongue, lips, eyes, hands, feet
or ankles, wheezing, difficulty breathing or swallowing,
hoarseness.

Risk of cardiovascular problems including **DEATH***,*
especially in patients with heart disease. It is important for
your doctor to check your hemoglobin while you are taking
Epoetin. If your hemoglobin rises too high or too fast while
using Epoetin, serious problems may occur, including edema
(swelling of the hands, feet, ankles, or lower legs), heart attack
or heart failure, high blood pressure, seizures, stroke, blood
clots in your heart, legs, or lungs, other side effects." (41)

WOW! Perhaps instead of taking this medication you could look at what foods your consuming and make the necessary changes to put iron back in your diet.

Chapter 5

· ·

What Are the Health Ramifications for Humans, Other Species and Our Planet?

<u>Earth vs/Livestock</u>

According to Michael Pollan in his book "The Omnivore's Dilemma",

> *'The grass roots truth is, if the 16 million areas now being used to grow corn to feed cattle in the United States became well-managed pasture that would remove fourteen billion pounds of carbon from the atmosphere each year, the equivalent of taking four million cars off the road." (42)*

I am not suggesting everyone become a vegetarian or vegan because as we have learned, we can effectively feed our meat protein sources the old-fashioned ways without adding noxious gases to the ozone. Mr. Pollan further states:

> *"...pastures (like those of Joel Salatin of Polyface Farm) remove thousands of pounds of carbon from the atmosphere each year. Trees take in carbon too, but they store most of it in their trunks and branches. Grasslands however, store most of their carbon in their roots. When those roots die off and become humus, the carbon becomes part of the soil.*

Because of this, grasslands are great at reducing carbon in the atmosphere and fighting global warming". (42)

According to Peter Singer, a Professor of Bioethics at Princeton University:

"Nothing changes the face of the planet as much as the way we produce our food. Since that has such a big impact on the environment, on other people, and of course on billions of non-human animals you have to think of this as an ethical issue. You have to think of the choices that you are making in terms of what you eat as choices with ethical consequences. I think that's why we should regard this as one of the central issues. After all it's something that we all do two or three times a day". (43)

So far, you have read excerpts from Dr. John Gray's book about the effects of mineral depletion of our soil, the introduction of herbicides to our foods by Monsanto and Dow Chemical among others. You have also read about how processed foods and refined sugars are the enemy to our bodies (Dee McCaffrey).

Dr. Gray says in general, we cannot physically ingest enough fruits and vegetables to nourish our bodies, given the mineral depletion of our soil. Dr. Stephanie Senoff clearly states in her interview with Jeffrey Smith (Chapter 2), the health risks are enormous when ingesting glyphosate, the active ingredient in Roundup herbicide. Dee McCaffrey states in her book, we're experiencing "Food Chemistry Gone Mad." (44)

Honey Bees and "Colony Collapse Disorder", Fiction or Truth?
So now, let us talk about what happens when food chemistry meets Mother Nature's creatures, the *butterflies, birds and the bees.* The following article posted on Huffington Post in 2013 by Evaggelos Vallianatos tells a harrowing story of what we're doing to our precious honeybees.

"In my 25-year experience at the US EPA, nothing illustrated the deleterious nature of 'pesticides' and 'regulation' better than the plight of honeybees. Here is a beneficial insect pollinating a third of America's crops, especially fruits and vegetables, and we thank it with stupefying killing.

Poisoning of honeybees became routine in the mid-1970s with the EPA's approval of neurotoxins encapsulated in dust-size particles that took days to release their deadly gas. Some of my EPA colleagues denounced such misuse of science and public trust. They told their bosses those encapsulated neurotoxins were weapon-like biocides that should have no standing in agriculture and pest management. Indeed, one of those EPA ecologists discovered the neurotoxic plastic spheres in the honeybee queens' gut. This meant poison in the honey. EPA acted with fury. It forced the scientist out of his laboratory and into paper pushing in Washington. Approval of the industry's neurotoxins expanded to cover most major crops. This meant honeybees had less and less space to search for food without dying. The blow-back of this almost criminal policy is the massive death of honeybees all over the country.

Government officials and industry executives cooked up an obscure name, "colony collapse disorder," to cover up the

pesticide killers of the honeybees. Meanwhile, the mission of
EPA of protecting public health and the environment almost
disappeared. I don't mean that EPA acted on its own out of
callousness or indifference for honeybees. No. Industry used
Congress and the White House in perverting EPA, making
it alien to its noble purpose. That's why EPA had no trouble
in adding more neurotoxins against honeybees. It 'registered'
the German neurotoxins known as neonicotinoids. Just like in
the mid-1970s EPA said yes to known deadly substances for
the convenience of farmers and for the profit of a handful of
chemical companies, EPA repeated its misguided policy in the
early 2000s. Now the neonicotinoids are spreading death to
honeybees all over America and the world.

I have known about this tragedy for some years, but
I always hoped honeybee keepers and reasonable farmers
would minimize the harm. I was wrong. A few days ago,
I called up a beekeeper inviting him to an environmental
conference planned for June 2015. He declined because,
he said, there would be no honeybees left in another year
or two. I was stunned. I asked him to explain. 'Scientific
evidence mounts almost daily confirming the decades-
long observations of beekeepers that pesticides are playing
a major role in the dramatic decline of honeybees and
other pollinators," he said to me. 'Singled out for special
condemnation is the neonicotinoid family of pesticides,
systemic neurotoxins which are the companion technology
of genetically modified crops and which have contaminated
hundreds of millions of acres. Characterized by some as 'The
Plutonium of Pesticides,' they are pervasive and pernicious;

persistent in the environment with half-lives of years. 'These products,' he continued, 'are water soluble and migrate readily with ground and surface water to be taken up by non-target plants [weeds, crops] at toxic levels, and if the research of some [scientists] is accurate, the effects on insects' nerve synapses are cumulative and irreversible, which means that there is no safe dose, however small. Exposure,' he concluded, 'as low as one tenth of a part per billion can be fatal to honey bees.' A part per billion is like pouring an ounce of chocolate syrup in 1,000 tank cars of milk. Yet such minuscule amounts of certain chemicals kill organisms like the honeybee.

The beekeeper, who prefers anonymity, is right on the deadly effects of neonicotinoids. He was angry and eloquent in describing the pesticide calamity all around him. He remembered the encapsulated neurotoxins and said he used to find 'piles' of dead honeybees. 'But,' he said, 'My honeybees recovered then. Now there is no place for them. I resent taking care of my honeybees only to discover they disappear or to see them dead. I speak to the state and federal elected officials and they pat me on the head and do nothing.'

As for EPA, only the word agency is true in its name,' he said. Talking to this deeply wounded beekeeper, I relived countless memories from my work. Listening to my colleagues citing data, cases of deadly results from allowing farmers to spray their crops with neurotoxic chemicals. Yes, honeybees are insects. But they give us honey, a divine-like food. Honeybees are also extremely valuable because they make

some of our food possible. Moreover, they are behind those
gorgeous wildflowers.

A world without honeybees would be unpleasant and
sterile. Add to that rising temperatures and you have a
nightmare world. Not only would such a world have less food,
it will surely be more toxic for all life, including us.

The tragedy of my beekeeper friend is American tragedy
written large. Time has come to say no to the poisoning of
our world. In a civilized society, there should be no chemical
warfare anywhere, particularly in raising food."(45.)

I recently heard a local reporter state that the current bee
population is down 42 percent from last year (2014).

The Monarch Butterfly

In an article from the Los Angeles Times, February 25th 2014, by
Louis Sahagun:

"Limits sought on weed killer glyphosate to help
monarch butterflies.

With monarch butterfly populations rapidly dwindling,
a conservation organization on Monday asked the U.S.
Environmental Protection Agency to implement tougher
rules for the weed killer glyphosate — first marketed under
the brand name Roundup — to save America's most beloved
insect from further decline.

In a petition, the Natural Resources Defense Council
argued that current uses of glyphosate are wiping out
milkweed, the only plant upon which monarch caterpillars
feed. The loss of milkweed is having a devastating effect on the

life cycles of the large, fragile orange-and-black butterflies,
which migrate through the United States, Canada and
Mexico.

It takes several generations of the insect scientists know
as Danaus plexippus to make the round trip because each
monarch lives only a few weeks in the summer.

Since federal glyphosate rules were last updated a
decade ago, its use has spiked tenfold to 182 million pounds
a year, largely due to the introduction and popularity of corn
and soybeans genetically modified to resist the herbicide, the
petition says.

The tenfold increase in the amount of glyphosate being
used corresponds with huge losses of milkweed and the
staggering decline of the monarch, Sylvia Fallon, an NRDC
senior scientist, said in an interview. 'We are seeking new
safeguards desperately needed to allow enough milkweeds to
grow.'

California's monarch population has fallen
an estimated 80 percent over the last 15 years due to
urbanization, drought, weed abatement programs and
pesticides, according to the nonprofit Xerces Society,
a Portland, Oregon based organization dedicated to
conservation of invertebrates.

The caterpillars are about 2 3/4 inches long, with a pair
of black antennae-like appendages at either end of a body
ringed with black, yellow and white stripes. They spend

most of their three weeks of existence munching on milkweed leaves.

The EPA is scheduled to complete a new review of glyphosate rules in 2015. But 'given the rapid decline in monarch numbers, the EPA should take immediate steps to review and restrict glyphosate's uses', " the petition says. "

The EPA *Helps*

"The petition asks the EPA to consider preventing the use of glyphosate and other weed killers along highways and utility rights of way where milkweed could grow freely without interfering with maintenance or emergency crews.

It also asks that farmers be required to establish herbicide-free safety zones in or around their fields, and urges the EPA to ensure that any new safeguards on glyphosate don't lead simply to more use of other weed killers that would be equally bad for monarchs and may pose health risks." (46)

"The good news is that butterflies are resilient and can rebound quickly,' Fallon said. 'All they need is milkweed on which to lay their eggs.' "(47)

The following information is taken directly from the EPA website:

"Convene a workshop with experts in plant pathology, atmospheric chemistry, and entomology to discuss the effects of ground-level ozone on the interaction between the Monarch butterfly and the milkweed plant. Prepare a synthesis paper of the findings and discussions at the workshop for dissemination to EPA program offices, regional offices, the scientific community, and the general public. Research needs will be articulated in the synthesis paper.

*The U.S. Environmental Protection Agency's (EPA's)
National Center for Environmental Assessment (NCEA)
within the Office of Research and Development (ORD) has
the responsibility to conduct ecological risk assessments to
assess the potential impacts of anthropogenic contaminants
in the environment. At an EPA-sponsored workshop plant
pathologists and physiologists, biochemists, atmospheric
chemists, and entomologists discussed how ozone may be
effecting the interaction between the milkweed plant and the
monarch butterfly. The monarch butterfly has an eastern and
western migratory route. Along both migratory corridors,
the common milkweed plant is relied upon by the feeding
butterfly's larval stage for nutrition. Ozone has been shown
to alter the nutritional quality of milkweed and many other
plants at concentrations commonly found in ambient air. The
scientists plan to develop a synthesis paper that will address
the potential for negative consequences to both the plant
and the butterfly. The scientists will also take steps toward
developing an integrated monitoring network across the U.S.
that will begin to provide data on the potential impacts of
ozone on the milkweed plant, the insect, and the interactions
between the two species".* (48)

Please note that nowhere in their workshop do they talk
about the roll that *glyphosate* has in destroying the milkweed
that monarch's feed on. They are essentially blaming it on
the destruction of the Earth's ozone layer, not glyphosate. In
addition, in their mention of the ozone layer, nowhere do we
find a discourse about the scientifically proven reasons for global

warming and the destruction of the ozone layer. In fact, some of the main reasons for the destruction of the ozone layer and global warming are intimately intertwined with the way we "grow" cattle, burn our forests and strip our land of minerals. Of course, all of those activities have a monetary attachment to our government and corporations that spend *millions* buying lobbyists, government officials and misinformation advertising in order to make *billions* at the cost of our and the planets health. When do we stop using harmful insecticides?

"As monarch butterflies plummet, it's time to rethink the widespread use of our nation's top weed killer. Today NRDC is calling on EPA to re-examine the widespread use of glyphosate, commonly called Roundup, in light of its impacts on monarch butterflies. Glyphosate was last approved by EPA in 1993 before the adoption of genetically modified crops that are tolerant to its use, known as 'Roundup Ready' crops. Now, however, Roundup Ready corn and soy dominate the agricultural system and the use of glyphosate has skyrocketed tenfold to 182 million pounds annually. As a result, milkweed – which is the sole food source for monarch butterfly larvae – has all but been eliminated from farm fields across the Midwest.

At the same time that spraying of glyphosate has soared, the monarch butterfly population has been plunging. This winter the population at their Mexican wintering grounds fell to just a tenth of its running average, to 33.5 million, and a calamitous drop from a high of one

billion monarchs in 1997, the year after the first Roundup
Ready crops were introduced to the market.

Because of this alarming decline, researchers this
year declared the monarch's migration is at 'serious risk of
disappearing.' This means we are in danger of losing, in just
a few short years, a marvel of nature that has existed for
millennia. The monarchs' annual flight from a tiny area of
Mexico to as far as Canada and back, all in a single season
and spanning several generations, is a unique phenomenon
still mysterious to science.

Although other factors like temperature and drought
also affect the monarchs, researchers broadly agree that the
widespread use of glyphosate in association with genetically
modified Roundup Ready crops has been a major contributor
to the decline of the monarch population. With glyphosate,
says leading monarch expert Karen Oberhauser of the
University of Minnesota, 'We have this smoking gun.'

Now that we know that glyphosate is having a
devastating impact on one of the world's most spectacular
natural wonders, it's time to restrict the pervasive use of this
and other weed-killers.

The EPA has the authority to conduct an urgent
review of any herbicide and impose restrictions to address
its adverse impacts. That's why NRDC has filed a petition
asking the EPA to undertake such a review of glyphosate and
develop measures that would reduce its impact on monarch
populations. Some of the measures we propose include
preventing use of glyphosate and other weed-killers along
highways and power-line rights of way where milkweed, a

relatively short plant, could grow freely without interfering
with maintenance or emergency crews – and requiring
farmers to establish herbicide-free safety zones in or around
their fields, or create other milkweed-friendly habitat. And we
encourage the agency to explore other safeguards to protect
monarch habitat from glyphosate and other herbicides.

The devastation of the monarchs is a disheartening
example of the many unintended consequences we suffer from
the industrialization of the agriculture system. By taking
steps to save the monarch, we must also take a hard look
at the wider impacts of our current land use and farming
practices. There are several other herbicide-resistant crops in
line for approval that will only further contribute to the loss of
milkweed and other native plants that pollinators depend on
unless we build in appropriate safeguards.

Though seemingly delicate, monarch butterflies are
remarkably resilient and their decline can be reversed – but
for that to happen we must find a way to make a little room
for the very plant that they need to survive". (47a)

The LA Times:

"The effects of GM glyphosate resistant crops could
affect different species, depending on their feeding and life
cycle requirements. The authors noted that, in the results
of their model, 'Skylarks showed very little response to the
introduction of GMHT rape. By contrast, the consequences
of introducing GMHT sugar beet were extremely severe,
with a rapid decline, and extinction of the skylark within 20
years. This contrasts with the cirl bunting, which showed

little response to the introduction of GMHT beet, but severe
consequences arose as a result of the use of GMHT rape.'

Similarly, the decline of Monarch butterfly populations
in North America since the mid-1990s has been linked
(in part) to the use of glyphosate-containing herbicides
on GM maize and soya crops. However, this is not due to
direct toxicity of the herbicide to the butterflies. Monarch
caterpillars are very dependent on one species of plant,
the common milkweed, as their primary food source.
Monsanto's guidance for farmers specifically mentions that
its glyphosate-containing herbicide Roundup Weather MAX
'will provide suppression and/or control of....milkweed,
quackgrass, etc' (emphasis added). Common milkweed plants
have been lost at very high rates from fields of glyphosate-
resistant crops, and it is estimated that common milkweed
has been largely eliminated from 100 million hectares of US
cropland following the introduction of glyphosate-resistant
crops. While not directly toxic to the butterflies, the use of
glyphosate interrupts the caterpillar stage of their life cycle."
(49)

I learned some time ago about the *real* relationship between
plants and birds. The next article really opened my eyes in a very
new and exciting way to the synergy between all living things on
this earth.

Dan Carlson on Music for Plants

The following is a portion of an article from a 2006 Biotech News
newsletter:

"When Dan Carlson's time was up after his second go-around with Uncle Sam, he took his honorable discharge and headed for the University of Minnesota, where he enrolled at the University's Experimental College to begin studying plant breeding. His first objective was to see if he could develop some kind of growth stimulant for plants so that greater yields might be realized. The product not only had to be low cost, but it also had to be effective for farmers and gardeners who worked the poorest of soils. Rather than trying to get nutrients to the plant by having to rejuvenate the soil In the long run, Carlson himself admits that soil remediation is the best answer, however this would be a huge and expensive undertaking for many parts of the world, requiring not only a lot of materials and manpower, but also a tremendous amount of time. Carlson reasoned that it might be more effective to try a more direct route: using a method of foliar feeding where the nutrients and growth stimulators would be applied directly to the leaves of the plant.

Plants have many tiny openings on their leaves called stomata ['Stoma' means 'mouth' in Greek-Ed.]. The 'stoma complex' is made up of two 'guard cells' which surround the pore, or stoma. The guard cells have the ability to open and close the stoma. Although the number varies from plant to plant, stoma range between approximately 500-1000 per square inch of leaf surface area. It is through these microscopic stomata that plants exchange gases with their environment. They 'inhale' carbon dioxide and 'exhale' oxygen and water vapor, for example. As Carlson was to discover, they can also absorb nutrients.

It wasn't long before he had come up with an organic foliar feeding solution which enables him to get significant growth rates in about three out of every hundred plants he tried. Carlson was on the right track; but the challenge was to find a way in which he could get a higher percentage of plants to 'accept' his product. If he could only find a way to get the plants to "breathe" better, a way to stimulate the stomata into action, then he might have a higher rate of success.

Carlson, still wondering how he might find a way to stimulate plant stomata, serendipitously came across a copy of Dr. George Milstein's (a retired dentist and avid horticulturist who recorded plant stimulating sounds called 'Growing Plants Successfully at Home') record. This set him to thinking in a direction which eventually led to the answer the stomata to open. He was later to discover a combination of frequencies which in fact did just that. What happened next was quite a surprise...

Stomata-Stimulating frequencies now in hand, Carlson collaborated with a Minneapolis music teacher by the name of Michael Holz in order to produce a cassette tape in which the sounds would be embedded in a recording of popular music. Although he didn't at first realize or even suspect it, Carlson later discovered that his special frequency combination was something which was anything but unique to him. Within just seconds of hearing Carlson's special sounds, Holz's trained ear immediately recognized the pitch to be a kind of sound he had heard many times before. Carlson's frequencies *turned out to be very similar to the frequencies and harmonics of birds as they sing their songs beginning just before the sun rises each day! According to authors Peter Thompkins and Christopher Bird, 'Dan Carlson had instinctively hit upon frequencies that were the ideal electronic analog for a bird Choir.'*

All of a sudden, it made perfect sense to Holz. 'It was thrilling to make that connection,' he said. 'God had created the birds for more than just freely flying about and warbling. Their very singing must somehow be intimately linked to the mysteries of seed germination and plant growth.'(50)

You can read more about Dan Carlson's *successful* experiments, Nobel Peace Prize recommendation and his invention "Sonic Bloom", which is still being sold today at Dancarlsonsonicbloom.com.

So we know that there is an obvious connection between birds and plants, why is it such a stretch to think we humans wouldn't be connected on a deeper level to our environment? Were we put on Earth just to suck the life out of every living thing, as if we are passing through this life without any responsibility for the consequences of our actions? I guess that's a rhetorical question but when I think about many of the CEOs of large corporations, moving through life as though nothing matters but the bottom line, it really pisses me off!

In the basic teachings of the Buddha, he taught that the first truth is that nothing is lost in the universe. Matter turns into energy, energy turns into matter. A dead leaf turns into soil. A seed sprouts and becomes a new plant. Old solar systems

disintegrate and turn into cosmic rays. We are born of our
parents; our children are born of us.

His teachings suggest we are the same as plants, as trees,
as other people, as the rain that falls. We consist of that which
is around us, we are the same as everything. If we destroy
something around us, we destroy ourselves. If we cheat another,
we cheat ourselves.

Let us stop cheating ourselves, and leaving our food choices
up to our politicians and corporations. If you really want health
for yourself and your loved ones, you MUST take individual action
and vote with your forks AND knives.

More food for thought: Everything on the planet is here
for a reason. Each of us, along with birds, bees and all the other
species on the planet *are supposed to* have a symbiotic relationship
to care for the planet in some way. If our only connection to
the planet and everything on it is ego based, we will perish. Our
species, particularly in the USA, is becoming increasingly sick and
diseased. The past 400 years have seen 89 mammalian extinctions,
almost 45 times the predicted rate, and another 169 mammal
species are listed as critically endangered.

*"Science is organized knowledge, wisdom is organized
life." -Immanuel Kant*

If we as a species cannot organize our science, we will not
have the benefits of wisdom to organize our lives or our planet.

Chapter 6

You CAN Afford to Eat Right

You may be thinking by now that your only hope to eat healthy in the current food environment is to win the lottery, buy an island, and build a bubble over it to prevent Roundup from blowing into your organic crops. Things do seem bleak when we look at the facts about the global spread of glyphosate (Roundup).

The Dirty Dozen and The Clean Fifteen

The best you can do, given the current environment, is to make small changes to your pantry by making a concerted effort to shop the perimeter of your store. What this means is to get fresh produce whenever possible, and do not buy produce listed on the "dirty dozen".

> *The fruits and vegetables on The Dirty Dozen List, when conventionally grown, tested positive for at least 47 different chemicals, with some testing positive for as many as 67. For produce on the 'dirty' list, you should definitely go organic unless you enjoy consuming chemicals.*

The Dirty Dozen list includes:

Celery

Peaches

Strawberries

Apples

Domestic blueberries

Nectarines

Sweet bell peppers

Spinach, kale and collard greens

Cherries

Potatoes

Imported grapes

Lettuce

As much as possible buy produce on 'The Clean 15' list. These foods bore little to no traces of pesticides, and are more safe to consume in non-organic form.

The Clean 15 list includes:

Onions

Avocados

Sweet corn

Pineapples

Mango

Sweet peas

Asparagus

Kiwi fruit

Cabbage

Eggplant

Cantaloupe

Watermelon

Grapefruit

Sweet potatoes

Sweet onions" (51)

Why are some types of produce more prone to sucking up pesticides than others? Richard Wiles, senior vice president of policy for the Environmental Working Group says: 'If you eat something like a pineapple or sweet corn, they have a protection defense because of the outer layer of skin. Not the same for strawberries and berries.'

The President's Cancer Panel recommends washing conventionally grown produce to remove residues. Wiles adds: 'You should do what you can do, but the idea you are going to wash pesticides off is a fantasy. But you should still wash it because you will reduce pesticide exposure.

Remember, the lists of dirty and clean produce were compiled after the USDA washed the produce using high-power pressure water systems that many of us could only dream of having in our kitchens." (52)

The full list contains 49 types of produce, rated on a scale of least to most pesticide residue. You can check out the full list from on the Environmental Working Group's website at: www. foodnews.org.

Cheap Food, Expensive Health

According to Drew DeSilver at the PEW Research Center, in his article, Chart of the Week: Is Food Too Cheap For Our Own Good? (51)

- *In the 1930's American spent about one quarter of their disposable income on food.*
- *Today less than 10 percent of American's disposable income is spent on food.*
- *...as the real cost of food goes down, each dollar we spend buys us more calories than it used to.*
- *According to U.S. Department of Agriculture data, the average American's total calorie intake rose from 2,109 calories in 1970 to 2,568 calories in 2010, -the equivalent of an extra steak sandwich every day.*
- *More than 78 million U.S. adults or 34.9 percent were obese in 2011-2012 – more than twice the rate found in a 1976-1980 health survey.*
- *We're already eating more fruits and vegetables.*
- *51 percent of people in a 2009 survey study reported exercising regularly, up from 46 percent in 2001.*
- *Americans, as a whole, also ate more fresh fruits and vegetables in 2010 than they did in 1970 (though again, that varies considerably among differing age groups).*

While the research for these statistics may be sound, I believe the conclusion to be over simplified in the face of our knowledge of what is actually in our foods today. The simple fact is that what most Americans think they can afford today is processed GMO foods that keep them physically addicted to consuming more and more of those same "foods," thus becoming obese and diseased.

According to the USDA website on Food Plans for September 2014, the monthly cost to feed a 1 year old on a thrifty plan was $94.80 vs a liberal cost of $176.70. The monthly cost to feed an adult male between 19-50 years old was between $188.30 and $374.50 and a female in the same age range was between $167.10 and $331.90. (52)

Somewhere in between those numbers, I hope you can find a comfortable place in your food budget for *real* health and nutrition.

We've been caring for my aging (88 years old) mother for about a year and one of the things I insist on is providing her with organic, non GM foods. She had been eating processed, GMO foods for many years and has many maladies as a result including IBS, heart disease, high blood pressure and depression among other things. Since being on a healthier regimen for about a year, her IBS has **greatly** improved, her balance is better and she doesn't require as much of her anti-depressants.

"Let food be thy medicine and medicine be thy food"
- Hippocrates.

It is not as simple as eating more fruits and vegetables and adding fish or quinoa to your diet. Becoming a vegetarian or a vegan is not necessarily the answer for every BODY; although there is strong evidence that has proven that substantially lowering your meat intake will lead to better health for you and the planet. For more information on vegetarianism and veganism, read "Diet for a New America" by John Robbins.

To really enjoy optimum health, you must also read labels to insure you are not eating anything with glyphosate or other potential insecticides, staying entirely away from processed foods, and limiting or eliminating the "Dirty Dozen" food list. Most foods that are non-GMO have a small rectangular label that reads "NON GMO project verified" nongmoproject.org.

Fast Food at Home

You may be thinking, oh those health food stores are frequented by a bunch of tree hugging hippies. (Do they still call us hippies?) I can't be seen in one of those places. What will my friends think? I can't give up my cheese burgers, fries, sub sandwiches or pizza! Here's a thought; make your own fast food right at home, using healthier substitutions for the processed and fast foods. Buy grass fed non-GMO meats, cheeses, potatoes, vegetables etc.

You will find that your body will not crave more than it needs since you will not be digesting sugars and other harmful chemicals that activate your "eat more" responses. Try substituting liquid stevia for your normal sugar, coconut oil for canola oil, and coconut or almond milk for dairy milk. All of these things take a little getting used to but are so worth it. Your cells will be doing a happy dance! Don't you deserve the best food that's available? I'm not talking about caviar and lobster, just good, whole, real food.

Starting about twenty years ago In my efforts to eat healthier on a budget, I decided to start making large quantities of soups, marinara or spaghetti sauces and anything else I knew my husband and I enjoyed eating. This took some time in the kitchen, about one day a week (my days off), shopping, chopping and preparing, then portioning labeling and freezing. Some dishes were more successful than others were, and I still enjoy experimenting with different combinations, even though not everything comes out exactly the way I planned. If you are on a *really* tight budget, maybe you should stick with proven recipes. Even the recipes that call for lots of processed and unhealthy ingredients can be made organically and/or healthier.

It isn't that we're not already carrying around toxic glyphosate in our cells, because it _is_ omnipresent, but more about how to decrease our continued ingestion of it, and other toxins in the food chain.

I know this may seem daunting, but we have to take a pro-active stance on our health if we are to thrive in an atmosphere of greed, narcissism and dis-ease. Instead of trusting all your immediate health problems to traditional medical doctors, consider looking up a naturopathic physician or homeopathic remedies. Unfortunately, most insurance companies do not cover these alternative modalities for health but after an initial consultation, your average cost for an office visit will range from $25.00 to $75.00, plus the cost of labs and nature-based remedies. Those numbers change according to where you live of course. In my small town of Prescott, AZ (approx. 50,000) it's *fairly* affordable. It's been my experience that the initial cost of these alternative medical practices is well worth it in the long term, as I don't have to continue to take pharmaceuticals that have the potential to destroy healthy bacteria or have harmful side effects. That's not to say that I don't believe in the benefits of Western

medicine. I would be dead now without some of their surgeries!
Just don't close your eyes to alternative medicine.

Dr. Susan Godman Interview

My next interviewee is Dr. Susan Godman. Dr. Godman became
discouraged, working as a nurse in conventional medical settings
with the typical patient presenting symptoms, doctor writes
a script' scenario. Looking for a better way to create health,
she went back to medical school looking for a more successful
approach. She found it in Naturopathy. With a perfect blending
of healing modalities and a wide scope of practice, she has the
tools to truly help create total wellness. Dr. Godman on GMOs and
processed foods:

> 'They're unleashed now. We're not going to stop a
> rolling ball moving downhill. It's already in motion and
> there's nothing we can do about it. Labeling is not addressing
> the real problem. We have to boycott. The diseases that
> I see in my practice all boil down to processed foods. The
> more man hands mess with a molecule, the more messed
> up it becomes. Our gut mucosa recognizes real food, and it
> recognizes what we had to eat in the Garden of Eden. What it
> doesn't recognize is a highly processed refined thing. We have
> immune cells all along the gut mucosa and those gault cells
> feel, literally like little feelers along the digestive tract that
> feel what we ingest. They "ask" is this something I have to be
> aware of, do I have to build up an immune response against
> it, or can I welcome it in, take it as nutrients, and actually do
> something with it? Food is information.

The stomach, I think, is our first brain. There are more serotonin receptor sites along the digestive tract than the whole rest of the nervous system combined. It really is the first brain. If you've got very intelligent cells scoping that stuff out and there is a whole lot of stuff coming down that number one is not food, it's not good information, and number two it's bad information, you're not getting the nutrient content that you need to build healthy new cells. You're also getting a lot of garbage information that is telling your cells the wrong thing. In response, your body builds up an immune response to it, and you have inflammation moving throughout the entire body, not only the digestive tract.

I had a young man come to me a few weeks ago from southern California. I don't know how he heard about my practice, but his father brought him in because he had psoriatic arthritis and was very sick. At just 23 years old, he was crippled with his disease. We started talking about his diet and he related to me that he worked for a contractor and drove through McDonald's every morning to get an Egg McMuffin and some kind of California burrito. It's even got French fries in it! For dinner he had a piece of steak (non-grain fed) and either a baked potato or fries with it. All we did was clean up his diet and do some drainage remedies, and he's been symptom free for three months.

He was ready to go on methotrexate, as prescribed by his doctor because he was in so much pain. He was going to have to quit his job and go on disability, at 23!

It's gotten so bad that about 80 percent or more of the patients I see have some kind of digestive issue. I tell them it probably has something to do with your gut and it's no surprise to them because they already have GI symptoms.

Our youth are getting more information about foods and many are very passionate about the situation. These are the people who are going to run our country in the next twenty years so education is very important.

So where are we going with all this and what do we do? At this point the tiger is out of the cage and there's really nothing we can do about it. They've GMO'd salmon, corn, soy and the list goes on and on. Once you have an organism out there, that organism is going to have sex with every other organism it comes into contact with. Within about twelve generations of that organism, you have absolutely NO non-GMOs. It's not a matter of avoiding them, but more about trying to stay alive while we mutate.

I'm sorry to be a dooms -dayer but they're using E-coli as the carrier organism to change the plant DNA. That's why it's called an organism on the part of DNA. People don't get that part! They think they're talking about the plant but they're really talking about E.coli. That's what gets in to move intracellular into the plant DNA.

If you've got an organism that's common in every organism but you get outside of that particular species, it creates disease. So if we get into contact with cow E.coli, we get very sick and can die from it. If you've got a lot of cells that already have the expression of E.coli, your immune system is going to be numb to E.coli and it won't recognize that organism when it attacks you. What that means is that we're going to have a wide-spread epidemic of disease from something very simple that will probably wipe out about 80 percent of the population.

I did my master's degree in France and found that in Europe, there's a lot of research on intracellular organisms or micro psalms like Lyme disease and spirochete. These are not viruses, but fully intact cellular organisms like a bacteria. They're small enough to live inside a human cell. Just like Lyme disease and other co-infectants talked about here in the US, it's become almost illegal to diagnose Lyme disease unless you use a specific test called the Western blot, which is less than two percent accurate. It's like going into a forest and looking for deer. If you don't see a deer you say there's no deer there, even though there may be fifteen standing all around you, out of sight. But if you do see a deer you can say, okay there's a deer. The Western blot test goes into your forest and says, I don't see any spirochetes, so I don't know what your problem is, but it's not Lyme disease. If you can't diagnose it as Lyme disease you're not legally allowed to treat for Lyme disease.

In Europe they have identified about 57 organisms as intracellular parasites. Here in the US, even at alternative medical conferences, it's taboo to even talk about this or test for it. They've even outlawed the microscope used to find them!

I've always questioned why they're working so frantically to hide these living organisms. Of course, it's about money. The bottom line is it's making us vulnerable and will wipe out a great portion of us.

There's no non-GMO corn to be found in the US, so if you're eating or have ever eaten these GM foods, you're in a mutating stage. So, how do we deal with this now that it's out? The key is to try to keep your children mutating as slowly as possible and help their DNA keep up with what their original cellular structure was, without being overrun.

At the end of the bad sci fi movie, most of the population will be wiped out and only the fittest will be around to take over.

I was a microbiologist before I became a naturopath, and know how organisms spread. They are information to our bodies and we can either take them as nutrient information and continue rebuilding and mutating with it, or our bodies can take them as a total attack and build up a huge response, having nothing but inflammation. Then we die of the inflammation and related diseases.

Naturopathic medicine has been around for 140 years, much longer than Western medicine. Before that, we had Shamans and medicine people. Now the dollars and prestige are wrapped up in allopathic medicine. There's a shift for people, now that they're not getting any better by taking more pharmaceuticals, to pay out of pocket for alternative medicines. Now that people are learning that changing their diet and health patterns and using naturopathic and homeopathic medicine actually works, they're forgoing their insurance company telling them what they can do and getting real, long term health."

Cancer Cells, Friend or Foe

I knew that we all have cancer cells in our bodies but was unaware that cancer cells could be good or had a beneficial use in our cellular structure. According to Dr. Godman:

> "Cancer cells per-se are not unhealthy, they're cells that are doing a particular job. You just don't want them running amok. It's just like in society, you're going to have butchers and bakers and candlestick makers. Suddenly your butchers say, 'I've got a cleaver and I'm going to chop up all those candles or hack up people. There's nothing wrong with that because I have a cleaver." They take on their own identity, go off, and start ruling the body. That's what cancer can do in the wrong environment. It's not because they're malicious, it's just that that's what they understand and they're being fed and nurtured by an unhealthy diet".

I guess it would be like comparing them to fire fighters. When the fire fighters aren't fighting fires, they're out in the community digging fire breaks, cleaning brush and educating the public about how to be fire wise. They're not just sitting around the firehouse waiting for the bell to ring. So if God gave us cancer cells, it wasn't just to make us sick but to do good as well. Everything has a purpose!

Chapter 7

Eat Right to Feel Right

Many of you are not used to exercise on a regular basis, and I totally get that, especially if you are not at your healthiest or have issues with your weight. You may have joined a gym in the past just to find that you have wasted your money and only walked in the door one or two times. You feel like the "odd man out" because of all the gym rats in spandex and tank tops giving you the hairy eyeball.

Processed Foods vs Weight Loss

The truth is it doesn't matter how many miles you put on the treadmill, stair step machine etc. If you're still consuming processed, GMO foods you'll most likely regain the pounds you lost at the gym after all that work. And you *will* get sick eventually! You may be a good-looking corpse, but what fun is that?

Conversely, if you are obese, you're probably addicted to processed foods and will always be hungry, no matter how much you eat. Even if you were to start going to the gym tomorrow, following a rigorous workout schedule, you wouldn't enjoy optimal health while still ingesting "non-foods". Your cells are literally starving to death!

Glyphosate vs Serotonin and Tryptophan

According to Stephanie Seneff:

"Tryptophan is one those amino acids that is clobbered by glyphosate. It's already deficient in your food because the food's been exposed to glyphosate. Then the gut bacteria would be producing tryptophan for you but they can't do it because they've got glyphosate contamination. So now, you have a tryptophan deficiency and worse than that, you end up with all these toxic gut bacteria pathogens and so your body launches an immune reaction to them. The body sends in macrophages to kill those bacteria. Those macrophages are going to be using a dangerous arsenal, so they need to have protection against that. The protection that they get is actually from Tryptophan. They produce something called kynurenine from the tryptophan and they hoard it. So they gather up all this kynurenine in order to protect themselves from the weapons they're releasing to kill the bacteria. So the small amount of tryptophan that's there is being sucked up by the microphages. By the time you get to the blood, there's very little tryptophan left and tryptophan is the sole precursor to serotonin, and serotonin is an appetite suppressant. So now, you have low tryptophan, low serotonin and high appetite....

So essentially the blood is not getting enough tryptophan to protect the cells of the immune system because the immune system will suck it out to protect itself against the glyphosate contamination. When the blood doesn't get enough tryptophan, there's not enough serotonin produced to suppress the appetite. So when your body isn't producing enough serotonin to suppress the appetite when you've essentially had enough to eat, your body will still crave more food. Recent studies have proven that low serotonin levels are directly linked to obesity. 95 percent of our body's serotonin is found in the gut. Serotonin is an extremely important neurotransmitter and is a well-known contributor towards feelings of well-being, sometimes also called the 'happiness hormone'. Even those who become more disciplined and lose weight will still have difficulty keeping the weight off until their serotonin and tryptophan levels improve." (23 b.)

Basically, if you're eating processed, GM foods, you're eating a LOT of glyphosate and will NEVER have normal healthy gut bacteria. Our local "GMO Free Prescott AZ" project sent away a water sample to a Canadian lab to test specifically for glyphosate. The results came back with an alarming .05 percent in our drinking water! (53)

As modern science and ancient Ayurveda has shown us, your gut is your second brain (or first depending on who you talk to). If neither brain is functioning properly due to glyphosate contamination, how can you possibly hope for health?

Melanie Banayat: To Give or Not to Give My Kidney

My friend Melanie, an author and holistic health coach told a story about her brother who was in stage four kidney failure resulting from poorly managed diabetes. He chose to go the medicinal route, treating his symptoms, rather than reversing the disease by eating differently. She said she watched him go through the medicinal route without any real signs of recovery or even a possibility of being managed without a kidney transplant. When he called to tell her that he needed a new kidney, she responded by telling him he had to prove to her that he was willing to change his diet and lifestyle before she was willing to give her kidney to someone who didn't care about it as much as she did. Melanie said this was a moral decision and had very much upset her to have put restrictions on a potentially lifesaving transfer to her brother. She always felt that if a family member needed something this important, she would instantly say yes. The problem was that she knew how he lived and what his food choices were. When they met for lunch with another sibling to discuss the potential transplant further, she watched what he ordered and ate. His continued choice to eat unhealthily made the difficult request for her to be his kidney donor that much easier to decline. I didn't ask what the outcome for her brother was but have to wonder if he ever saw the recklessness of his choices.

After having rheumatoid arthritis for years Melanie was able to treat herself through changing to organic, non-GMO foods and eliminating nightshades from her diet, among other things. It only took six weeks for her to feel the relief of symptoms in her hands and about a year for the symptoms in her feet to completely disappear. Not everyone has allergies to nightshades but many people do.

Having been a health nut for about twenty-five years, I can honestly admit that I have never been obese or particularly unhealthy. I always felt like I was dodging the proverbial bullet when it came to having severe problems. I have, however, had a complete hysterectomy and gallbladder surgery.

Post-Surgery Instructions

After my gallbladder was removed via emergency surgery, I asked my doctor what dietary changes I should make, given that I no longer had the gallbladder to process "gall" from my liver. Amazingly he said no changes were necessary! Really? Something about that did not ring true to me so I asked my naturopath the same question. It was a kind of DUH moment. Of course, you have to make changes to reflect the removal of a once very important organ.

This is just another example of Western medicine vs alternative medicine when it comes to understanding real nutrition.

Blood flows through all regions of our body. It brings nutrients and waste from cell to cell. The liver acts as the main filter for this blood and it is the main eliminator of waste in our body. Its job is to remove all forms of waste, including dead blood cells and toxins. The waste product that is created as a result of the Liver cleansing out toxins is bile, which is being manufactured at all times. Not being wasteful, the design of the human body actually has a use for this bile other than simple elimination. Bile is the main substance responsible for the breaking down of fat in the digestive system. The gallbladder is the organ that receives the bile from the liver and stores it until it is needed in the digestive system to break down fats and cholesterols.

Pre and Probiotics

In Western culture, the gallbladder is usually removed when infected or partially blocked, as a burst gallbladder is a MAJOR health risk. The removal of the gallbladder will result in a lack of smooth flow between the liver and the individual's fat digestion. Most individuals who have had their gallbladder removed will need to either watch their fat intake, or balance their fat with bile supplements and enzymes. What my naturopath recommended, among other things, was to lessen unhealthy fats, eat unctuous soups, particularly in the winter season, and balance my fat intake with bile supplements and digestive enzymes like a good probiotic.

A good probiotic supplement can help replenish your body's good bacteria and naturally help to support digestive and immune health. The word probiotic comes from the Greek "for life", and it refers to friendly bacteria that live naturally in the gut. Probiotics promote good digestion, facilitate the absorption of nutrients, boost the immune system, and help prevent an overgrowth of harmful organisms in the digestive tract.

Most probiotic food is fermented, at least partially. A short list of probiotic food choices includes miso soup, some soft cheeses, yogurt products like kefir, sauerkraut and many pickles. However, it is difficult to know how many live bacteria are in these foods and how much will reach the digestive tract. By using a supplement, you have a more accurate measure of what and how much you are getting.

Many people who think probiotic food is beneficial are now also taking a prebiotic supplement or eating foods that naturally contain prebiotics. The best-known prebiotics are Fructo-oligosaccharides - which you will find in the abbreviated form (FOS). These naturally occurring carbohydrates are found in certain foods, such as bananas, honey, onions, tomatoes and wheat (organic, non GMO). Prebiotic foods include goat's milk, honey, Jerusalem and regular artichokes, oats and many fruits. Fructo-oligosaccharides cannot be digested or absorbed by humans, but support the growth of good bacteria. Put simply, prebiotics feed the 'good' bacteria in the gut.

If you are serious about getting and staying healthy, change the way you look at yourself first. It isn't about being skinny, it's about being healthy! Exchange the processed, GMO foods you put into your God-given vessel with food the way God intended it to be, nourishing and filled with the earth's love and abundance. Be patient with your progress, health does not happen overnight! When you fall off the health wagon, do not beat yourself up by giving up. Have compassion for yourself and start again. You deserve health and happiness!

Chapter 8

· ·

Healthy Brain Cells and Decision Making

You read in the previous chapter, 95 percent of our body's serotonin is found in the gut. If we have gut dysbiosis due to glyphosate contamination, our brain does not receive enough serotonin and tryptophan to function properly. Our receptors are not getting the message to stop eating, feel calm, listen to our better judgment (or even have good judgment at all), have feelings of contentment, compassion, inspiration, and community.

<u>Food Toxicity and Anger</u>

The other sides of this are feelings of not being a part of anything greater than ourselves, feelings of lack, self-loathing, anger, frustration, depression and suicidal tendencies. It's hard to wrap my brain around the fact that toxic insecticides and herbicides with origins from a war more than 50 years ago can be a main contributing factor in why people in our world, mostly in the US, are so diseased and angry. The anger I would understand, if people were actually angry about the contamination of their food sources, but the sad fact is that most people don't even understand why they are angry. And the vicious cycle continues!

Low serotonin levels are also associated with violent behavior. People with lower serotonin levels become irrationally violent and are unable to reason about the consequences of their actions (Think about all the public shootings). Some of my own grandchildren are suffering from this aberrant behavior. This is very difficult for me to talk about because it is so close to my heart.

Christopher
One grandson, now 25, is in prison, basically for poor judgment and lack of impulse control. He didn't kill or hurt anyone, embezzle millions from shareholders, get caught for insider trading, bank fraud, counterfeiting, or any of the "white collar" crimes that get people a slap on the hand and sent to minimum security vacation prisons. Like many inmates, he ended up in prison because of the 3 strikes rule. Don't get me wrong, I don't condone stealing in any way, but his punishment does NOT fit his crimes.

He was diagnosed with ADHD at about age five. From the time he could walk and talk, he was always on the move and nonstop talking. It wasn't until he was registered for kindergarten that my daughter was told he had a problem. His teachers and principals said that due to his inability to sit still or be quiet, he needed to be evaluated for possible ADHD, with emphasis on the hyperactivity.

He was taken to a psychologist and my daughter tried non-medication options (behavior modification). Within a few very short months, the school insisted that she look at possible medications that would allow him slow down and be able to learn better. By the time he was in the first grade, he was on Ritalin.

It seemed to work for a while, but he was still struggling with his energy level and not being able to sit quietly. He was put in the special education class by the third grade and we were starting to see side effects from the medication (headaches, loss of weight, lethargy, nausea and angry outbursts).

My daughter was forced to start changing his meds to try new drugs, Concerta, as well as Adderall and antidepressants. By the time he was in the sixth grade he was stealing (impulsive) and had mood swings. My daughter decided to give him drug holidays (when not in school, no meds). It wasn't until he was in his late teens that he stopped taking the medications and started having some self-control, although he is still impulsive and talks a lot.

For most of his life, he has been in weekly counseling and special education at school as well as CFT's (Child and family team meetings, behavior modification in class) and required close parent teacher relationships.

This is a classic example of the scenario I wrote about in chapter one, where the parent starts out eating what they believe to be good food (or at least affordable). Their children eat those same foods and the long and short of it is, they cannot function normally because of the chemical and pesticide contamination of those processed foods and the insidious effects on the body's cells.

Melissa Fields Interview on Brain Integration Therapy (BIT)
The following interview is with Melissa Fields, a brain integration therapist:

> *"It's hard to control what we're eating. Take for example the kids. I pack my kids lunch every day before they go to school and put in lots of healthy options. They may trade it*

to somebody else. They trade their roasted seaweed snacks for the pudding cup. It's very difficult to control what we eat in this country because there are so many bad choices unless you're educated. I think there is a complete lack of education about food, which makes it very hard to make choices about trying to control what you eat. Unless somebody is teaching the kids, what to eat then they become a generation that hasn't been taught about real food. Then they teach their kids what to eat and that's all wrong too. That's already happened in our country. There's been a complete lack of education for so many years that we're several generations into bad eating habits.

Speaking of the schools, when I was teaching we had a grant based on providing the students healthy foods. Supposedly the Food and Drug Administration was supposed to regulate what schools provided under the grant guidelines. The menus that were approved included fruit cocktail which is full of high fructose corn syrup. When parents sent their kids to school and thought they were getting balanced meals at school, they were just being fed complete crap. The teachers don't know what to teach because they aren't educated about food themselves. It just becomes this complete lack of education and support, which leads to all of our health problems.

I didn't know a lot about GMOs until recently. I didn't realize how few people know about them even though they've been around for 20 or more years. I think perhaps as you decide to become aware of food there are graduated levels of it. GMOs might be at a higher level of understanding, like when people know they should eat fruits and vegetables, but then find out they should be eating organic fruits and vegetables. They probably don't even realize what organic means besides the absence of pesticides. Once I started learning about GMOs, I realized how completely asinine the situation is. Why would anyone blend animal genes with corn? That just doesn't make any sense, especially because according to the research I've seen, there is no added benefit. It doesn't actually promote added resistance to pesticides. There's not any real research that shows that they've had any benefits. There are certainly no health benefits, in fact quite the opposite. They were trying to make crops that were more hardy and resistant. Even that hasn't happened. In fact farmers just have to use more pesticides so it just compounds the problem. It's just crazy!

Part of what I ask clients when they come in, is if they're willing to make environmental changes, because some people just aren't. For example, children coming in with ADHD. Some parents just want their child to get fixed and they don't want to have to do anything different to support the child or even modify their child's diet. I think that's the mindset of our quick fix society in general. I have had several clients who are very serious about their child's health and they really want to help. Sometimes it has to be a graduated kind of plan because they're going from eating the standard American diet of fast and highly processed foods every single day to trying to tell their child to eat broccoli, brown rice, and some kind of salmon for dinner. When they're used to eating McDonald's you have to use a more graduated plan. I don't tell them to take out everything all at once, but to start by trying to take out most of the refined sugar. That gives them the highest benefit in the shortest amount of time. Then I recommend they adjust down, eliminating processed foods over time and introducing 'real' food in their place. I think the average person thinks sugar is just in candy bars and desserts. They don't think about it in the juice box or cranberry juice or the cranberry juice cocktail. Those have zero percent real juice.

For instance, I had one little boy who had been through my brain integration technique and he had improved, but there were still some issues like lack of concentration and poor sleep habits. Fortunately, his parents didn't want to put him back on his medication. We set up a graduated program for the next 30 days to try to eliminate as much sugar as possible. Then try to get him onto a diet without processed foods. We incorporated some other things like essential oils but the primary focus was on diet and getting him to eat real food. It was difficult because of school, grandparents, and other people in his environment who didn't support the new plan. He had a really strong mother who was very helpful, very assertive, and an advocate for him. You really need that in today's culture. To tell his teachers, 'No I don't want him to have a cupcake at school when it's a kid's birthday.' She was awesome about that. It took about three months of cutting out the sugar, and then as they cut back on the processed foods they could see bigger and bigger improvements. She ended up switching his other siblings to the same foods and then to

*organic, and then gluten free because even the siblings saw
how well he was doing.*

*Over a period of several months, he was healthier than
everybody else in his family was. When everybody in the
house would get sick, he didn't. They started thinking maybe
this is something we should all do. The dad was probably the
most resistant of all. He was fine with everybody else eating
well, but he didn't want to change his habits because he grew
up eating in certain ways. I don't know if he stayed with it as
well as the rest of the family, because he would go to work and
go out to lunch.*

*There's a balance of not wanting your children to feel
deprived at home or school, but his results were drastic. The
teachers felt like he was a completely different child.*

*From my own experience as a teacher, I think you
would see the result of the child and know that a lot of it
has to do simply with diet. Then you start thinking maybe
I shouldn't allow cupcakes in the classroom or maybe I
shouldn't be buying fruit snacks. He was an awesome
example. I've had other children go through the same thing,
just in varying degrees of success according to what their
support system is at home. To be at your optimal potential
you have to be looking at your diet".*

I had the opportunity to go through brain integration
therapy (BIT) with Melissa, and was amazed at the results that I
saw and felt after only one of my seven treatments. I initially went
to see if the therapy would help me to better focus on writing this

book. Within the first 24 hours after my first treatment, I was writing with fervor and continued to do so.

Brain Integration Therapy is an effective way of correcting the neuropathway blockages in the brain that can be the root cause of such problems as dyslexia, emotional control issues, PTSD, ADD/ADHD, and the debilitating after-effects of certain head injuries, especially post concussive syndrome (PCS). BIT is a drug-free, non-invasive solution that affects not just academic performance but all aspects of life.

I have since written my grandson in prison to tell him of my findings and strongly suggest that he consider the treatment after his release next year. Along with any alternative therapies, he will of course have to completely alter his conceptions of what a healthy diet is. Even with BIT, if he doesn't change to a processed food free, GMO free nutritional eating plan, he won't experience the benefits long term.

The new modalities of treatment available today outside of Western medicine and pharmaceuticals are truly inspiring and amazing. I encourage everyone to research alternative methods of correcting whatever maladies you may be experiencing. I do acknowledge that Western medicine has its place in the human health arena but it is certainly not the be all - end all.

Our brains are made of the fats we consume. So it stands to reason that if we're consuming fats that originate or are permeated with GMOs, glyphosate, or other harmful chemicals, our brains are also going to suffer the negative effects of those substances. Healthy, whole dietary fats are fundamentally important for a healthy, whole brain. Our brain does not care what kind of carbohydrates we eat; it just wants and needs them to survive. All carbohydrates break down into sugar but our problem is eating the wrong kinds of sugars. In the absence of eating the right non-GMO foods, a healthy brain is unable to synthesize enough neurotransmitters and begins to function as if it was damaged. When the brain is provided the good carbohydrates necessary for optimal function, we can expect to live a more normal existence. We are less likely to suffer from depression, suicidal tendencies, over eating and ultimately obesity.

We must cut back on the intake of unhealthy carbohydrates, especially refined, processed sugars. Pastas, below ground vegetables and their derivatives (potato chips etc.) in large quantities can also prove very damaging to healthy brain cells. That doesn't mean an occasional baked potato is out of the question, just not a steady diet of them. And of course any processed GMO foods which we know contain high levels of glyphosate among other harmful man-made chemicals.

Leslie McKeown Interview

The following interview was with Leslie McKeown, of GMO Free Prescott, a non-profit organization educating people about the health risks of eating GMO foods.

"If you have a special needs child you have zero time for yourself. How do find a balance and how do you make those changes that are important? I go to the grocery store and I look at people with babies in their carts, and I look at what's in their carts and have to bite my tongue. I want to tell them, you are poisoning your baby; it ought to be against the law. You don't have to buy everything organic. I have what I call

*the high risk things and the low risk things. I always go to
lectures with an example of; well this is 'off the shelf' pasta
sauce that has no GMOs in it. It's not organic, but there's
no GMOs in it and you can buy it for $2.69. Your chances
are much better buying that, than buying the cheaper, GM
brand. Save your money there, by buying ready-made sauce
and buy the organic pasta, peppers, meats etc. Buy a huge
bag of blue corn chips at Trader Joe's for $2.50. There is no
excuse for buying the processed, GMO corn chips.*

*I began eliminating GMOs from my diet after joining
GMO-Free Prescott, two years later the health benefits are
noticeable and numerous, they include: healthier digestion,
increased energy, better sleep and decreased seasonal allergies
and colds. I was already purchasing primarily organic whole
foods so my food costs did not increase that much. In fact they
decrease as I eliminated the few processed foods I purchased.*

*After noticing the healthy changes we experienced it
occurred to me to changes my pets diets as well. I have a
13 year old dog with chronic allergies that often escalated
to pneumonia several times a year. After switching to a
GMO-free kibble and canned food the episodes have almost
disappeared and his overall well-being is much better. The vet
said he looked like a much younger dog! We also adopted two
feral kittens who had been fed a traditional commercial diet of
GMO food. Within a week of changing their diets to GMO-
free, their diarrhea cleared up and they had more energy and
were much happier. The slight cost increase of GMO-free food
is completely offset by the decreased vet bills!"*

Chapter 9

Can This All Be Fixed?

Green Spirit Farms, Milan Kluko Interview

The final interview was with Milan Kluko, CEO of Green Spirit Farms. I am so impressed by the new technology he has brought to the field of growing organic foods:

> *"I feel that the less processed our food is, the better it is for you. That's an easy position to take but I believe that. Part of that less processing starts with trying to add diversity in what we grow because obviously we do a lot of mono-crops and mono-culture. When we do those things, it sort of puts Mother Nature on the side-lines. The way that agriculture is done now is obviously mono-culture. So its corn and soy beans. In order to get yield, you have to produce more food per acre.*
>
> *We need to have less processed foods and more fresh fruits and vegetables, which is what I do, obviously, and the best ways to grow food. I'm not necessarily talking about organic or non-organic foods sources. Just the way we grow food. We occupy a lot of land with mono-cultured grown food and that's just how it is. I think there is something to be said about doing it the old way.*

I have two children and you can see how kids think what food is, and it is not about I do not like broccoli or carrots; it is more about I'd rather go to Burger King than McDonald's. From a cultural standpoint that is the first thing you notice. Food is often talked about as a location, not about food. What can I get at McDonald's, what can I get at Burger King? I think that's a big part of the issue. In addition, when you look at what that food has historically been like, obviously, there is not a lot of green in it and it is processed. Anecdotally, from a health standpoint, you look at childhood obesity, diabetes and all those things and it is an issue.

Fast food growing up for us was very rare location wise. Going out to a restaurant that, wow, am I going to get a great meal, and that meal is going to be a few courses. So it was still about a social experience and the nutrition was not paid attention to because the meal was more of a destination than the experience of eating to nourish ourselves. 'We' don't talk to our kids a lot about food either.

One of the things that we did when we started Green Spirit Farms was that we have a non-profit called 'The Earth Campus', that does community outreach with education, not necessarily preaching education, but when we bring in the Kindergartners through sixth graders, they get to see what we do from a vertical farming perspective. They're sort of amazed. We also show them the differences between growing food outside on an acre which gives you 'this much' food for spinach, this much kale, etc., and here's how much water it takes, and here's how much land it uses. At Earth Campus, we talk about where food comes from and how it all should be local. We are part of an agricultural system that operates inside now because of new technology. When you think about it, fast food is only available because of technology.

Back in the early days of fast food, it was not that fast and there wasn't anything innovative about it. Basically someone else was just cooking a hamburger or hot dog for you and the 'fast' was 'add French fries.' No, now you've got the microwaves and flash-frozen foods. What we do at Earth Campus is try to explain the agricultural cycle, the ecologic cycle, we talk about nutritional food and part of the tour is they get to taste it. And that tasting is what's important because then they can go to the grocery store to the produce section and see different types of Green Spirit Farms lettuce that they've already tasted and liked, vs the sugary cereals and the candy. So now they have a personal experience with real food and they know where it comes from.

The reasons I started Green Spirit Farms was, first, Eco Systems Performance for our agricultural supply chain. Very simply put, we should not be eating lettuce grown in California if you live in Chicago. Second, is that that system of eating uses up land and water in California. So, for me it was more about reducing our carbon footprint. I often believe that if I can't have lettuce or spinach during the winter time, then I have to try to find another source. When I grew up people used to can food. Of course, we don't see much of that anymore because of the burgeoning frozen food market.

So we have trucks running down the interstate, delivering produce from California to Chicago, Philadelphia and New York 24 hours a day, 7 days a week because of

convenience. Then we have airplanes flying in fruits and
vegetables from other countries because we want oranges in
January. And we want raspberries in March!

Our vertical system of growing uses about 1 percent
of what is now being used to grow leafy greens. This goes
back to ecosystem system performance. Your food basket is
bigger because you can make it more regional, expanding
in the winter time. We don't use plows or tractors, thus
lowering our carbon footprint further. We keep our beautiful
basil plants alive, rather than cutting them, for nine to ten
harvests making it more sustainable. Our leafy greens have
about 10 to 12 times less sodium content than those you get
from California, just because they're using irrigated water
with a chloride buildup from over forty years of farming the
soil. About a third of their water evaporates leaving behind
chloride.

We're doing some experimentation right now with
growing raspberries inside in our farm in Michigan. We've
already grown strawberries inside in Michigan and we're
working with the California farms that sent us some of their
raspberry plants to see if we can grow them in our system in a
longer term study.

Food sovereignty is something I feel very strongly
about. We need to be able to work with the local farmers and I
consider myself a local farmer. They're selling their tomatoes,
peppers, etc. I talked to a local farmer and asked them what
would you do if you didn't have to grow your raspberries
outside? The farmer has about a month and a half to make all
of his or her money. That particular farm I visited has been

working their farmland for about 40 years and their parents worked it for 60 years before that. They had a very rough winter (in the Midwest) that killed many of their raspberry plants.

What I'm doing is feeding into that agricultural system saying, gee, if I can grow raspberries and strawberries locally, rather than have them 'imported', great. I know I can grow spinach, kale, lettuce, radishes and those kinds of things, but I don't grow tomatoes because I've got other farms around me that grow those in their season. I start planting my tomato plants at the end of August so they're ready in December. That keeps the local tomato farmer alive. That is food sovereignty. I'm growing food where the people are at, not trucking it across the country. Not only has the new technology gotten better, but also we have an appropriate use of that technology.

We like to have our vertical farms within one hundred miles of a major metropolitan area because that's what the truck farmers did.

Plants are a living and breathing carbon based source, just as we are. Whether or not we're more evolved than a plant remains to be seen. Our plants like music and we have a 'playlist' at our farm that starts in the morning with a little Vivaldi, evolves into Motown, then a smattering of different classic rock favorites. We found that the plants do not like rap. In the afternoon, the plants get a quick dose of Sinatra, late 60s early 70s Beatles, Eric Clapton and some late 90s 2000s. Music is all about vibration and the humans and plants like that because we can hear the water running in our vertical growing stations, cascading from the top down, water falling back into the reservoirs. The lights come on slowly around ten AM, mimicking the sunrise because like us, plants need time to relax in the evening.

We work with the University of Arizona, Purdue University and Michigan State University as a consortium to learn more about how we grown vegetables. They're looking at this as a much bigger play in the future of agriculture because those are traditional agriculture schools. U of A already has an indoor controlled growing environment. I'm teaching them vertical farming the way we do it here at Green Spirit Farms.

These farms can run on solar. We can use geothermal for cooling and heating. The full spectrum lighting that we use provides a lot of our heat source and in the middle of Michigan in the winter; our electric bill is around $500.00 per month." (54)

How can we as a country do anything to eradicate glyphosate and harmful pesticides from our food sources, when we continue to be undermined at the highest levels? The conflict of interest between Justice Thomas and Monsanto should concern us all. May 31, 2013 by Ilyssa Fuchs:

"Supreme Court justice Clarence Thomas, a lawyer for Monsanto, refused to recuse himself from the case brought against Monsanto by farmers in 2013:

About two weeks ago, the Supreme Court ruled in favor of Monsanto, when it held that a farmer had violated their genetically modified soybean patent. In short, a farmer purchased genetically modified soybean seeds from

*Monsanto, subject to a licensing agreement, which allowed
him to plant the seeds for one season and one season only.
Subsequently, the farmer engaged in a process that replicated
the seeds, and was able to harvest and save some of his
own genetically modified seeds for the next season. When
Monsanto found out, they sued the farmer for infringement
of their patent. In response, the farmer raised the patent
exhaustion defense, arguing that, 'the initial authorized sale
of [the] patented item terminate[d] all patent rights to that
item.' However, **the Court disagreed**, and concluded that this
defense did not apply.*

*You might have expected this opinion to be written
by Justice Thomas, considering his ties to Monsanto.
Alas, the Court actually decided this one unanimously,
in an opinion written by Justice Elena Kagan. Thus, even
if Justice Thomas had recused himself from the case, the
outcome would have been the same. Nonetheless, considering
the possibility that other cases involving Monsanto could
and may come before the Supreme Court at some point in
the future, questions remain about Justice Thomas' conflict
of interest and his ability to remain impartial. Moreover,
although the US Code of Judicial Conduct does not apply
to Supreme Court justices, Justice Thomas' unwillingness
to recuse himself in cases involving his former employer,
Monsanto, is surely cause for concern." (55)*

Here's some good news, but keep checking out the site to see
how it all comes out.

California vs Monsanto

Monsanto Lawsuit in CA: (Natural News)

"A class action lawsuit coming out of California could deal another hard blow to the infamous Monsanto Corporation. The lawsuit is pointing out what - that glyphosate, the active ingredient in Monsanto's Roundup, is killing not only plants but also targeting specific enzymes in the microbiome of the human gut.

The more we apply glyphosate in agriculture and on lawns, the greater its residue in food products. Ultimately, glyphosate residue makes its way into our gut and kills important species of bacteria that we depend on to stay healthy. The good bacteria colonies are responsible for regulating our immune system and helping it respond to invading pathogens. These bacteria help the body break down nutrients and protect the gut wall from being penetrated by other toxins.

However, there is no mention of this science on Monsanto's Roundup labels. Entire countries approve glyphosate because they are not educated on how the herbicide destroys the human body from the inside out

Monsanto is lying straight up on labels that claim, 'Glyphosate targets an enzyme found in plants but not in people or pets.' That's what this new class action lawsuit is pointing out. Monsanto has been lying about the science all along. The lawsuit isn't making direct links between glyphosate and cancer, even though the World Health Organization recently confessed that glyphosate is a carcinogen. Instead, the lawsuit is pointing out the basic lie that Monsanto has been peddling all along, that glyphosate does not affect humans.

Monsanto's glyphosate lies impact practically everyone. The class action lawsuit, (Case No: BC 578 942) was filed in Los Angeles County California and alleges that Monsanto is guilty of using false advertisement when they say the herbicide is harmless to humans. This is no small matter. Glyphosate is the herbicide of choice throughout the world. Most of the genetically engineered crops in our world are made specifically to withstand this chemical. Labeling GMOs is not enough. Educating people on the action of glyphosate and proving that it harms the people as a whole is most important.

The lawsuit points out that glyphosate targets the EPSP synthase enzyme, which is found in human and animal intestines. If this enzyme is being wiped out over time, then humans and animals lose their ability to fight off disease. If the CDC is so concerned about the herd immunity of the human race, then why aren't they taking a stand to stop the mass application of glyphosate?

The lawsuit points out: 'Because it kills off our gut bacteria, glyphosate is linked to stomach and bowel problems, indigestion, ulcers, colitis, gluten intolerance, sleeplessness, lethargy, depression, Crohn's Disease, Celiac Disease, allergies, obesity, diabetes, infertility, liver disease, renal failure, autism, Alzheimer's, endocrine disruption, and the W.H.O. recently announced glyphosate is 'probably carcinogenic'.'

The world is awakening to glyphosate toxicity. The world is starting to wake to the toxic reality of glyphosate. Is this the beginning of the end for the herbicide? Just recently, The International Agency for Research on Cancer listed glyphosate as a Group 2A carcinogen. Even the American Cancer Society declared the herbicide a Group 2A carcinogen. In Beijing China, a resident named Yang Xiao-lu filed suit against the Chinese Ministry of Agriculture requesting the toxicology report for glyphosate when it was registered with the Chinese government. The Ministry responded by saying the toxicology report contained 'trade secrets.'

Delving further into history, we find that the US Environmental Protection Agency (EPA) stated in a memo dated October 30, 1991 that glyphosate was deemed a possible carcinogen by the agency in 1985. By 1991, the memo was changed, listing glyphosate as not carcinogenic, despite three scientists' refusal to sign the document. The data clearly shows that there was a significant increase in tumors in laboratory animals on glyphosate but since higher doses of glyphosate didn't render greater tumors, the EPA let the herbicide pass as not carcinogenic.

All this falsification of data is coming to light along with the fact that glyphosate is literally breaking down the human immune system by destroying specific enzymes in the human gut microbiome. Glyphosate is acting as a vector for mental disease by breaking down beneficial bacteria in the human gut, allowing other toxins to infiltrate the blood and bypass the blood-brain barrier." (56)

We hope that in time, Monsanto, Dow and the rest will be held accountable for all this. But now these big corporations are systematically buying out small and large seed companies in order to have total control of everything that is grown in the world! One last scenario or food for thought:

Let us say Monsanto continues on their greedy path and never has to make ANY effort to clean up the Glyphosate in the world and *it* continues to permeate every living organism.

Inevitability, those who can't afford to educate themselves, or to eat whole, clean foods become sick. They leave this earth much earlier than they would have, had they made changes in their food choices.

Many of the one percent population, who have for millennia used the services of those in the middle to lower income or class levels, no longer have those people to do their menial jobs for them because they're dead! Those jobs included planting, growing, tending and sowing the agro-crops they are 'feeding the world.'

Monsanto never cleans up their mess which results in the extinction of honey bees, monarch butterflies and birds among other species. There's no more clean water, except what people can save from the effects of global warming and the melting of ice in what used to be colder climates. The air isn't breathable because of all the toxicity and no vegetation to filter it. Sounds like a Sci-fi movie right? We'll call it "Welcome to Mutant Earth".

With all the overwhelming evidence that contradicts any evidence of progress, there is now a massive grassroots movement to make change. Authors like Steven M. Druker, Jeffrey Smith, and Deborah Koons to name just a few and organizations like

Slow Food USA.org, GMO Free USA, GMO Right to Know, the Center for Food Safety, Food Revolution Network, The Non-GMO Project, The Green Revolution and FMTV (Food Matters TV) are getting the word out to consumers all over the world. These authors and organizations are on a mission to help their fellow human beings become more aware of their choices for the health of their bodies and our planet.

The authors cited in this book are pioneers, taking risks to speak up against what is so obviously wrong with the business and political environment surrounding food in our world.

Maui vs Monsanto

In this article by Jon Rappaport, he talks about how:

> *"...the 2014, Maui SHAKA Movement and voteyesmaui. org won a temporary ban on new Monsanto/Dow GMO crops in Maui County. They proved that banning poison is more powerful than labeling it. Unfortunately, this was not the end of their battle against the poisons of Monsanto and Dow, but they got it right by going after them on a different level. They got down to talking about the poisons of Monsanto and Dow rather than the labeling of their end user products.*
>
> *It's a war against lying corporate poisoners. The GMO labeling ballot measures are really PR campaigns, and they keep some degree of awareness alive about GMO crops. They're not full educational campaigns, because the amount of teaching they do is superficial, despite their claims to the contrary.*
>
> *PR is slogans. Education is much, much deeper, and it certainly includes aggressive information about the*

horrendous effects of Roundup, among other GMO issues. So here's the point. If these GMO-labeling ballot campaigns are really PR, then why not redirect the PR against Monsanto and the other corporate criminals, instead of monotonously hammering away on "the right to know what's in your food"?

There's nothing to lose (after labeling defeats in California, Washington, Colorado and Oregon), and everything to gain. Monsanto is building this reality: GMO foods are wonderful and safe and the planet benefits.

So far, the counter reality is: Let Monsanto and their allied farmers grow their food, as long as the consumer can ID it on the label and reject it, if he wants to.

Take a few million of the dollars now being spent on pro-labeling campaigns and, instead, put it into video web ads that play all over the world:

For example: A destitute farmer (and his family) stands in front of his wasted, dusty, super-weed-choked field, states his name and says: 'I'm an American farmer. Monsanto lied to me and killed my farm and my livelihood with their poison called Roundup. And it doesn't even work. The weeds it was supposed to knock out are bigger than ever. Monsanto strangled my soybean crop. They ruined my farm. And my daughter is sick from the Roundup poison....'

Then....Boom. A few of your cold-eyed, take-no-prisoner attorneys stroll into the frame, and one of them looks into the camera and says, 'Hello Monsanto. Thinking of suing us for this ad? Bring it, baby.' A man pushes a large trunk on a dolly into the frame. He opens the trunk and takes out sheaf after sheaf of papers.

> *The attorney says, 'Monsanto? This is the evidence*
> *that shows you've been lying to the people about how safe*
> *GMO food is, and you've been lying about your poison called*
> *Roundup, see you at the first deposition. It's going to be a*
> *DOOZIE Monsanto.' A large red title appears at the bottom*
> *of the screen: BAN GENETICALLY MODIFIED FOOD. It*
> *fades out, to be replaced by another title: SEND MONSANTO*
> *CRIMINALS TO PRISON."* (57)

To Label or to Ban, That is the Question

Steven Druker states in his book 'Altered Truth, Twisted Genes':

> *"...now that people are generally more aware and better*
> *informed, it's important they recognize the key issue here is*
> *not that GE foods are on the market without labeling but*
> *that they're on the market at all – and that federal law would*
> *have kept them off the market if the FDA had not fraudulently*
> *broken it."* (58)

While I agree that at this point labeling initiatives are not as effective as they would have been twenty years ago, it certainly doesn't hurt to let the population know what they're consuming. At least they could lessen the impact of these toxins over the long run if they just had the information necessary to *avoid* buying the most toxic foods.

The DARK Act

The DARK act or Denying Americans the Right-to-Know can be partially summed up in the following excerpt from the article found on The Center for Food Safety website. Per Wenonah Hauter, executive director of Food & Water Watch:

'The federal government has failed consumers for years when it comes to GMO labeling, so people around the United States are getting labeling laws passed at the state level, it's no surprise that Big Food and the biotechnology industry want to use Congress to block state level efforts. But it's time for Congress to shine a light on GMOs and ensure that they're properly labeled.

'The biotech industry built its empire by deceiving American consumers,' said Ronnie Cummins, national director of the Organic Consumers Association. 'Now that consumers realize the extent to which they've been deceived, and the extent to which their health has been compromised by chemical companies masquerading as food companies, they are demanding transparency. HR 1599 is a direct attack on consumers' right to know the truth about what's in their food. It's also a blatant attack on states' rights and on democracy itself.'

'The DARK Act is profoundly undemocratic as it robs citizens of their right to vote for labeling of genetically engineered food,' said Andrew Kimbrell, executive director at Center for Food Safety. 'Citizens of 64 other countries have that right and Americans should as well. Congress needs to listen to the democratic will of the people, not the bottom line of Monsanto.'

Jim Goodman, an organic dairy and beef farmer in Wisconsin, added, 'It seems funny to me that, despite efforts nationwide to minimize the impact of big government, the DARK Act is exactly the opposite. Does it make sense that the

US House of Representatives would choose to dominate state and local laws around labeling GMOs?'

'Pesticide corporations and their allies in Congress are trying to keep Americans in the dark,' said Kristin Schafer, policy director at Pesticide Action Network. 'Americans have a right to know and a right to choose whether they want to support genetically engineered crops that promote increased and widespread herbicide use.'

Once again, this bought-and-paid-for GOP part of Congress has shown how little they care about the American people, and how willing they are to sell out the people.

And once again, you hear almost nothing about it in the media that want to keep the people as ignorant as possible so that they don't find out what goes on behind our backs." (59)

The article below by Paul W. Faust, is the most recent outcome of the vote on the DARK act in Congress.

"The Dark Act has been voted on in Congress, and every single Republican voted for it. The Dark Act is a bill that was written up by the people who supply this country the food it eats, and it says that food manufacturers do not have to tell you everything that is in that food, 'especially' when it comes to herbicides and other chemicals like the GMOs made by Monsanto. They can poison you and they do not even have to tell you about it.

How pathetically greedy do you have to be, and how stupid can you get, to vote for a bill that allows poisons in the very same food that they will also be eating? That pretty

much tells me that Republicans are even willing to poison
themselves as long as there is a good profit in it for them.

Remember this, voters: 'Every' single Republican voted
for this bill and against the best interests of the American
people. But that has become typical for a party owned by this
country's special interests and greedy rich." (60)

Some good news is that the war on Big Food is making its
mark in a BIG way and Big Food is taking a huge hit in revenues.
I found the following information in a Fortune magazine I picked
up at the doctor's office.

"An analysis by Moskow found that the top 25 U.S. food
and beverage companies have lost an equivalent of $18 billion
in market share since 2009." (61)

You get the gist of these messages right? If we don't educate
ourselves and *DO* something about the state of our current
food crisis, and I don't mean shortage because we know that's a
Monsanto myth, we deserve whatever we get. We all know that
nobody gets out of this alive, but big agro has been screwing
around with our food for so long, all we can hope for these days is
to "mutate" slowly toward old age. We owe it to our loved ones to
take good care of ourselves now, so that as we age, we don't inflict
our lack of health on those left to care for us. I see so many people
in their fifties, sixties and above that simply do not care enough
about their health enough to change bad habits. That puts an
enormous strain on families, finances and the health system.

If you have a child with Autism Spectrum or any of the
previously mentioned diseases, at the very least consider

changing to a processed free diet of fresh, organic fruits and vegetables, grass-fed beef, organically grown poultry, and wild caught fish (if you're a meat eater), or other healthy protein sources. Some of those would include quinoa, fermented organic soy beans and legumes, nuts (especially sunflower and pumpkin seeds for their whole proteins), organic dairy and sprouted whole grains. Even if you don't change to a 100 percent non GMO diet, you can expect to see a dramatic change in your loved ones just by eliminating processed foods full of GM corn, soy, rice, etc.

As I mentioned earlier, people who have children, particularly special needs children don't have much, if any, time for themselves due to the overwhelming tasks before them of caring for their loved ones. Consider this: If you could make just one change in your life and that of your loved ones that would lesson your burden and increase their quality of life (thereby increasing YOUR quality of life), would you make that change? What if that change is as easy as changing what your family eats?

That being said, don't let your brain write checks your body and budget can't cash. Set small, daily, achievable goals. Don't tell yourself you're going to go into the kitchen and completely clean out the fridge and cupboards of all processed, GMO foods unless you can afford to replace them right now. Just edit out the worst culprits, like refined sugars and any items that are full of corn syrup. If you have children or other family members in the household that you prepare foods with or for, talk to them about the changes you would like to happen. If you don't already know, ask them what foods they enjoy most that can be made without the use of processed, GM foods. Keep a supply of non-GMO, non-processed snacks in the kitchen for you and your kids.

I found a great brand of organic potato chips by Boulder that actually has only three ingredients, potatoes, olive oil and salt. Go figure! Be careful, they're addictive!

A dear friend of mine is not only a yoga instructor at my donation only yoga studio, he's a Cordon Bleu trained chef. Shortly before I moved my mom into our home last year, I hired him to start cooking weekly meals for her. I buy all the organic, non-GMO ingredients for her, based on what two or three meals she'd like that week, and he takes a few hours, once a week in her kitchen, to prepare and portion them out for her. Since she's been on this regular eating plan, she not only eats real food, but she's eating things she enjoys. All I have to do is heat up her meals. Before starting this plan, we thought she was on her last leg, ready to leave us in only a few months. Now almost a year later, she's feeling much better and seems to be enjoying life more. As I said earlier, I know none of us gets out of this alive, but at least we can have a better quality of life while we're here if we choose to educate ourselves.

Sign every petition that deals with getting rid of genetically modified foods that you can find. Write letters to your local and state politicians about your desire to have clean food. Keep voting from state to state to label (or BAN!) GMO foods. Even if you don't live in a state that is working toward the right to know, if you sit back and wait until the issue comes to your state, it will take so much longer to get a foothold. We absolutely have a right to know what we are eating.

To quote Steven Drucker: "The focus should expand from mere labeling to full elimination." (62)

Letter to Congressman Kucinich

In early 2001 my mother wrote a letter to congress, to Dennis Kucinich specifically, about her concerns with genetically engineered food. This was his response:

"I have many concerns about the health, safety and environmental impacts of introducing genetically engineered food into our food supply. I question the wisdom of releasing genetically engineered food, flies, fish, and trees into our environment without adequate safeguards to prevent unintended impacts. I advocate for a sensible and safe approach to genetic engineering. I follow the age-old wisdom that it is better to be safe, than sorry.

I believe American families should have the opportunity to choose what they eat because we just don't know the long-term impacts of genetically engineered food. For that reason, I have introduced the 'Genetically Engineered Food Right to Know Act,' which requires labels for genetically engineered food. I have also introduced the 'Genetically Engineered Food Safety Act,' Which requires strong safety testing before genetically engineered foods are placed on the market. I am also drafting more legislation to regulate other areas of concern. We are not alone in our concerns over the health and safety impacts of this technology. The British Medical Association has recommended that genetically engineered foods be labeled and the European Union, Australia, New Zealand, South Korea and Japan have required labeling of these foods."

Again, well over 14 years ago our individuals in government were aware of the possible hazards and unknowns of GMOs, but the lawmakers have done absolutely nothing. All that being said, the tiger really is out of the cage with respect to GMOs in our world, our food and the cells of our bodies. Let's take back our individual power and do something for ourselves. We *can* start to reverse some of the damage.

Read labels before you buy anything you put into your God given vessel or that of your loved ones. This is the only vessel with which we traverse our individual paths. What does your vessel contain? The tools to carry your spirit and soul to a fulfilling life, or the toxins to make your journey filled with pain.

If you frequently enjoy eating out, you may want to curb that habit. It wasn't that long ago that I truly enjoyed going out to enjoy a meal at one of our favorite restaurants. I know that my husband laments that I will no longer go out to eat, unless it's at "The Local", a new restaurant that my friend opened earlier this year. The only reason I'm willing to go there is that they buy local, organic produce, grass fed beef from less than four hours away, Non GMO chicken and most of their cooking ingredients are un-processed, and organic. That includes the sugars and flours they use for their pastries. I can only hope that other restaurants will follow suit. Given the transient nature of most restaurants, it would certainly be wise to follow the public's interest in better health, and their desire to know where their food comes from.

There is so much information now available on the internet that you would have to live in a hut without electricity not to know about what's going on in your world. It won't be long before all the "Dirty Little Secrets" are known everywhere.

I wrote this book with the intention of bringing more awareness to a subject that should be near and dear to everyone's heart, and brain, and liver, and stomach, and gall bladder! I hope for your sake that if you haven't already made necessary changes in your consumption of processed, GMO foods, that you at least consider looking further into the subject. While I've shared an overwhelming amount of what might be considered "gloom and doom," I sincerely hope that if you haven't already, please start to take an active role in your own rescue. Luckily for us, a plethora of books, DVDs, and documentaries are now available on the subjects put forth in this book.

"Health does not 'come from' independence or 'lead to' it.
Health is independence." - Wendell Berry (63)

Another Casualty

I must share one final casualty of our food system and toxic environment; my beautiful 23-year young granddaughter Jennifer drowned, after going to a court date in Camp Verde, AZ. She had been addicted to heroin for about five years and although she always wanted to get clean, and tried numerous times, she was unsuccessful. Most recently, she expressed a real desire to get clean, go back to school, make a better life for herself and make amends to her family.

She was a sweet young girl who loved people, especially young children. She was also a person prone to instant anger and lashing out when she perceived someone attacking, or berating her or those she cared for. She fiercely defended her family and friends.

Jennifer was beautiful and vibrant, intelligent, witty, and funny. She was also a child raised on processed, and GM foods. Her parents never knew until recently how these foods are slowly killing everything of value on our planet. As I shared in the first scenario in chapter one, along with Jennifer, several of my grandchildren are suffering the effects of these same toxic, inert foods. Her mood swings were seemingly out of her control, so she found solace in heroin. ADD, ADHD, OCD, depression, angry outbursts, addiction, and lack of impulse control are just a few of the indicators of food toxicity over several years and commonly begin manifesting in utero.

Again, I'm not suggesting that people shouldn't be culpable for their actions just because they've been eating inert food, and don't have the capacity to think about some of their actions throughout life. I'm just pointing out some of the other, possibly more obvious reasons now, that should be considered when placing blame.

As much as I thought the "Twinkie defense" (64) was ridiculous when it came out in 1979, in light of what I have learned about how our food affects us on a cellular level, I now have to re-think that position.

I recently went rafting with John and Ocean Robbins of The Food Revolution Network. Along with over thirty other like-minded people, we took four days to float down the Klamath River in northern California. This was the most meaningful vacation I have ever taken. My original purpose in scheduling this adventure was to let some of my granddaughters ashes go in the river, and get away from my very stress filled schedule. I thought that for the most part, I would be alone to release my sadness and stress.

What I found was a community of loving individuals that were willing to share their selves, and all the raw emotions that make up a life. We laughed, cried, and sometimes danced together.

What I received from this trip was a much deeper understanding of how we all connect to each other, and to our world. We connect through not only our food choices, but also how we perceive our place in a community. When we allow ourselves to receive the bountiful blessings of our own essence, our eyes and hearts can be more open to an awareness of our personal and global environments. We have a responsibility to our planet and ourselves to listen to the innate inner wisdom we all possess.

I have a greater understanding now of how I can make a difference in my small community. By speaking about organizations like Food Revolution Network and others, perhaps I can awaken something in others to help them to make better, healthier choices for their future.

I asked one of my spiritual guides during my yoga teacher training in 2009 how I could help my friend of twenty-five years with her stage-four stomach cancer. She had been addicted to sugar for most of her life and struggled with every diet available. When she had a Lap-Band surgically implanted on her upper intestine, she was successful at losing weight, but still ate the same processed, toxic foods and sugar. When her tests came back, they found that just below the Lap-Band her intestine was black with cancer. She lived exactly seven months after her diagnosis.

My spiritual guide told me that many people will die and that that is what had to happen before we awaken. At the time, I thought this to be callous, but now that I see the bigger picture, I find it very sad.

As soon as we are born (or at conception), we begin our life processes. We begin to experience lives with a family, sometimes without, with one or two parents, sometimes-good parents, sometimes not so good, and with or without siblings. If the best we can expect in our short time on Earth is a life of malnourishment and disease as a direct result of greed at the highest levels of our society, it begs the question of why we bring more babies into the equation at all. Many young people falling in love want to procreate, to share their love with children and build families. The fact is that many of them have incredible difficulty conceiving because of disorders in the reproductive organs due to ingesting processed and GMO organisms. With the current statistics of Autism, ADD, ADHD, OCD and myriad other abnormalities in the majority of children born today, it's a much more difficult choice for couples to make.

It seems like a crapshoot at this stage of our evolution, or de-volution as our current reality is revealing. As I said earlier in the book, I know none of us gets out of this alive, but what about experiencing a real quality of life while here? Our bodies were never designed to eat the crap that's now being touted as *natural* and healthy. How many millions of people will have to die a slow, painful death before we awaken?

To your health.

Appendix

1. If you can choose two subjects about the "dis-ease" in our country as it relates to our food sources, what would they be?
2. Why are these subjects your primary focus?
3. What are your thoughts on GMOs and processed foods in the world?
4. Without divulging identities, can you relate any first-hand knowledge about how our food quality has affected someone you know?
5. How do you think these issues can be resolved, or if they have been already, what was the/your protocol used to achieve and maintain health?
6. In your mind, what do you think needs to be addressed first and foremost with regard to educating the public about what they eat?
7. Do you think we are making any progress in our country on improving knowledge about how to be healthier? Please elaborate.
8. How do you feel about the efficacy of food apps (if you have knowledge of them) available to download onto cell phones such as GoodGuide, Fuducate, Locavore, Chemical Cuisine, and Food Facts.com?
9. Any other comments about your life's passion?

Interviewees

Dr. Heidi Hartmann-Taylor DC

Juliana Goswick - Yavapai County Big Brothers, Big Sisters

Melanie Banayat - Author and health and nutrition coach

Leslie McEwan - Former vice president of GMO free Prescott

Milan Kluko - Green Spirit Farms CEO

Melissa Fields - Brain Integration Therapist

Dana Murdoch - Former private practice rehabilitation counselor

Dr. Susan Godman - N.M.D.

Resources

Books

Altered Genes, Twisted Truth; Steven M. Drucker

Dinner at the New Gene Café; Bill Lambrecht

Diet for a New America; John Robbins

Food Fight; Daniel Imhoff

Food Inc.; Robert Kenner

Genetically Engineered Food; Ronnie Cummins & Ben Lilliston

The Mars & Venus Diet & Exercise Solution; John Gray, Ph.D.

The Omnivore's Dilemma; Michael Pollan

The Science of Skinny; Dee McCaffrey, CDC

Stretch Your Brave, Hack Your Story; Melanie Banayat

Superpigs and Wondercorn; Dr. Michael W. Fox

The Unsettling of America; Wendell Berry

Movies/DVDs

As we Sow; Jan Weber

Dirt: The Movie; Gene Rosow and Bill Benenson

Food Fight; Chris Taylor

Food Inc.; Robert Kenner

Food Matters; James Colquhoun and Laurentine ten Bosch

Forks over Knives; Dr. T. Colin Campbell,

Dr. Caldwell B. Esselstyn Jr., Dr. Neal Barnard

Fresh; ana Sohia joenes

Future of Food; Deborah Koons

Farmaggedon; Kristin Canty

The Garden; Scott Hamilton Kennedy

Genetic Roulette, The Gamble of Our Lives; Jeffrey M. Smith

Hungry for Change; James Colquhoun,

Laurentine ten Bosch · Carlo Ledesma

Killer at Large; Steven Greenstreet

King corn; Aaron Woolf

Origins, Our Roots, Our Planet, Our Future; Pedram Shojai,

Elmira Shojai & John Lasso, Well.org

Our Daily Bread; Nikolaus Geyrhalter

PlanEat: Shelley Lee Davies

Poison on the Platter; Mahesh Bhatt and Ajay Kanchan

Supersize Me; Morgan Spurlock

Symphony of the Soil; Deborah Koons Garcia

War on Health; Gary Null

References

1. Wendell Berry, The Unsettling of America; Chapter 5, page 74.
2. Genetic Roulette, Jeffrey M. Smith, Founder, Institute for Responsible Technology
3. Superpigs and Wondercorn" by Dr. Michael W. Fox, 1992, pg. 102
4. The Daily Mail; http://www.dailymail.co.uk/debate/article-2310267/How-genetically-modified-foods-disturbing-reality-lives.html
5. Superpigs and Wondercorn" by Dr. Michael W. Fox, 1992, pg. 31
6. http://frac.org/initiatives/hunger-and-obesity/why-are-low-income-and-food-insecure-people-vulnerable-to-obesity/
7. & 7.a Dr. John Gray, Ph.D., The Mars & Venus Diet & Exercise Solution
8. Dr. Linus Pauling, The Root of All Disease pg. 184
9. Thumb Butte Distillery, Prescott, AZ.
10. July 23, 2014 Mercola.com http://articles.mercola.com/sites/articles/archive/2014/07/23/cheap-factory-farmed-chicken.aspx
11. Dudley, Cash - FDA Fall Public Meeting: Cloning Issues Relating to Animals Raised for Food , November 4, 2003. http://www.upc-online.org/experimentation/102803ge.htm

12. Reuter's, online http://www.reuters.com/ article/2012/02/28/us-monsanto-lawsuit-idUSTRE81Q1PN20120228

13. Frederick Douglass, 1857

14. Food Safety Modernization Act # 7 Risk/Hazard Prevention

15. Huffington Post, June 9, 2014

16. Wikipedia

17. Huffington Post, June 4,2014

18. New York Times – Business Day April, 3, 2013

19. Natural News: (http://www.naturalnews.com/041464_glyphosate_Monsanto_toxicity.html##ixzz3PfqLlv89)

20. The Horrific Truth about Roundup, Mercola.com http://articles.mercola.com/sites/articles/archive/2013/06/09/monsanto-roundup- herbicide.aspx www.mercola.com

21. Genetic Roulette, by Jeffrey Smith. DVD, Video

22. http://www.fda.gov/AboutFDA/CentersOffices/Officeoffoods/ucm196721.htm, 22.a & b, https://en.wikipedia.org/wiki/Tom_Vilsack

23. 23a and 23 b. The Horrific Truth about Roundup, Mercola.com, Dr. Don Huber, Mercola.com, http://articles.mercola.com/sites/articles/archive/2009/11/21/France-Finds-Monsanto-Guilty-of-Lying.aspxIn 2009.

24. www.gmwatch.org, Claire Robinson interview

25. Is Drug-Company Money Tainting Medical Education? By Jeffrey Kluger Friday, Mar. 06, 2009, http://content.time.com/time/health/article/0,8599,1883449,00.html.

26. Network, 1976 Film

27. Michael Pollan, https://www.youtube.com/ watch?v=rbZBJT358_Y

28. Monitor liquid pesticide label. http://www.agrian.com/ pdfs/Monitor_4_CA_Liquid_Insecticide_Label.pdf

29. http://www.agriculturesnetwork.org/magazines/global/ mountains-in-balance/indigenous-knowledge-re-valued-in-andean written by Miguel A. Altieri

30. http://www.digitaldictionary.org/where-does-the-word-diet-come-from/

31. Dee McCaffrey, Science of Skinny Pg. 54, 55, 56, 57, 58

32. Dee McCaffrey, "The Science of Skinny" pages 102,3,4 and 131.

33. Dee McCaffrey, Science of Skinny, pg. 75

34. Dee McCaffrey, Science of Skinny, pg. 90

35. http://www.greenmedinfo.com/

36. Dee McCaffrey, Science of Skinny pg. 136

37. Dr. Weil, http://www.drweil.com/drw/u/QAA401181/Is-Carrageenan-Safe.html

38. Citation: Ronald Reagan: "Statement about Distribution of the Cheese Inventory of the Commodity Credit Corporation," December 22, 1981. Online by Gerhard Peters and John T. Woolley, *The American Presidency Project*. http://www.presidency.ucsb.edu/ws/?pid=43377

39. 39. By Jeffrey Kluger Friday, Mar. 06, 2009, http:// content.time.com/time/health/article/0,8599,1883449,00. html

40. http://tvtropes.org/pmwiki/pmwiki.php/Main/ UnreadableDisclaimer

41. Vaughn Aubuchon, http://www.vaughns-1- pagers.com/ medicine/prescription-drug-tv-ads.htm

42. Michael Pollan, "The Omnivore's Dilemma" Pg. 149

43. Peter Singer – Professor Bioethics, Princeton Univ. Planeat" movie www.planeat.tv

44. Dee McCaffrey "Science of Skinny" pg. 131

45. Evaggelos Vallianatos, Huffington Post Scholar and author of several books, including, "Poison Spring: The Secret History of Pollution and the EPA" (with McKay Jenkins), Honeybees on the Verge of Extinction, Posted: 11/25/2013 5:07 pm EST Updated: 01/25/2014 5:59 am EST http://www.huffingtonpost.com/evaggelos-vallianatos/ honeybees-on-the-verge-of_b_4326226.html

46. L.A. Times, February 25, 2014│By Louis Sahagun

47. & 47.a, Sylvia Fallon's Blog, NRDC (National Resource Defense Council), Posted February 24, 2014, http:// switchboard.nrdc.org/blogs/sfallon/

48. EPA website, http://www.epa.gov/

49. Copyright 2015 Los Angeles Times

50. Copyright 2006 – BIO/TECH Publishing, Ltd. – WWW. biotechnews.com, http://www.dancarlsonsonicbloom. com/. Awards: "Prestigious awards for great agricultural accomplishments" from the Japanese government; Humanitarian of the Year, "for his unceasing dedication to alleviating hunger, pain, disease, and sufferings for the Peoples in the world", Institute for Human Potential, 2002; Nominated for the Nobel Prize in Economics, 2001; 2002, 2003; American Biography; Honor of Dignity; Man of the Year, American Biographical Institute, 2004;

21st Century Award for Achievement, International Biographical Centre, 2004; Biographical entry in the American Biographical Institute's 2000 Greatest Minds of the 21st Century; International Biographical Centre's 2000 Outstanding Intellectuals of the 21st Century award; International Biographical Centre's 2000 Outstanding Scientists of the 21st Century Order of Excellence award, Nominated for Lifetime Achievement Award. Memberships: Honor of Dignity and Man of the Year 2003, American Biographical. International Biographical Centre's International Scientist of the year 2004, Dan Carlson -1941-2012

51. Drew DeSilver, Chart of the Week, PEW research Center, May 29, 2015. http://www.pewresearch.org/fact-tank/2014/05/23/chart-of-the-week-is-food-too-cheap-for-our-own-good/

52. USDA website, Official USDA Food plans, September, 2014.

53. http://www.cnpp.usda.gov/sites/default/files/CostofFoodSep2014.pdf

54. http://www.gmofreeprescottaz.org/

55. For more information on Green Spirit farms go to: http://www.greenspiritfarms.com/

56. The Forward Progressives website article: Ilyssa Fuchs

57. http://www.forwardprogressives.com/the-conflict-of-interest-between-justice-thomas-and-monsanto-should-concern-us-all/, Natural News; Monsanto Lawsuit in CA: Wednesday, May 06, 2015 by: L.J. Devon, Staff Writer http://www.naturalnews.com/049609_Monsanto_false_

advertising_glyphosate.html#ixzz3bYRUVHIS, Jon
Rappaport, Wednesday, November 5, 2014 Blog post:
http://www.thelibertybeacon.com/2014/11/06/election-
bang-maui-bans-gmo-crops-by-jon-rappoport/

58. Altered Genes and Twisted Truths, Steven M. Druker pg.
398, 399.

59. http://www.centerforfoodsafety.org/press-releases/3923/
over-300-groups-urge-congress-to-label-gmos

60. Paul W. Foust, Susquehanna Twp. in "The Patriot News",
August 04, 2015,

61. Fortune magazine issue 6/1/15 Beth Kowitt pg. 63

62. Steven M. Drucker, Altered Genes, Twisted Truths, pg.
398

63. Wendell Berry, The Unsettling of America, pg. 183

64. https://en.wikipedia.org/wiki/Twinkie_defense

Glossary

Hedgerow: an old English term that refers to narrow planting strips that grow along field borders, fence lines and waterways. In the Northwest, this ancient design method is being expanded to incorporate a diverse number of plant species with a wide variety of functions.

Hedgerows often consist of trees, shrubs, ground covers, perennials, annuals, and vines depending on the function, size, and location of the planting strip. The Functions of Hedgerows and Living Fences are to enhance wildlife. Hedgerows provide habitat for a large variety of mammal, bird, reptile, and insect species, many of which are beneficial predators of plant pests. Encouraging game birds can provide recreation for the landowner and a potential source of revenue. Other: Wildlife corridors. Nectar source: bees and other pollinators. Edge species that thrive where two or more habitats come together.

Statins: drugs used to control high cholesterol. Statins (or HMG-CoA reductase inhibitors) are a class of drugs used to lower cholesterol levels by inhibiting the enzyme HMG-CoA reductase, which plays a central role in the production of cholesterol in the liver, which produces about 70 percent of total cholesterol in the body

Off-label use: a prescription drug being prescribed for a purpose not listed on the product's label. This is a common and acceptable practice by doctors.

Acknowledgments

Thanks to Alison Donahower, my editor and Pam Israelson, my book designer. Jessica Holgate, for reading the first draft and giving me great feedback; my husband David, for helping with the first edit; Scott Mies, my fellow yogi and author for sharing his expertise in writing; Kerry Ott, for transcribing my interviews and Melanie Banayat, for sharing information on formatting and publishing.

Thank you David, for your loving support and patience over the past 24 years, through all of my creative endeavors. Thank you Jessica, for choosing me as your mother in 1969, and being my best friend and champion. Thanks to my mother who inspired creativity and compassion in me all of my life.

CPSIA information can be obtained at www.ICGtesting.com
Printed in the USA
LVOW07s2359201015

459068LV00011B/72/P